STAINES LIBRARY
TEL: 0300 200 1001

S

SURREY
COUNTY COUNCIL
WITHDRAWN FROM STOCK
AND OFFERED FOR SALE
WITH ALL FAULTS BY
SURREY COUNTY LIBRARY

SURREY

Overdue items may incur charges
as published in the current
Schedule of Charges.

L21

☑ THE CHECKLIST SERIES

MANAGING BUSINESS COMMUNICATIONS

First published in Great Britain in 2015 by
Profile Books Ltd
3 Holford Yard
Bevin Way
London WC1X 9HD
www.profilebooks.com

10 9 8 7 6 5 4 3 2 1

Copyright © Chartered Management Institute 2015

The moral right of the authors has been asserted.

All rights reserved. Without limiting the rights under copyright reserved above, no part of this publication may be reproduced, stored or introduced into a retrieval system, or transmitted, in any form or by any means (electronic, mechanical, photocopying, recording or otherwise), without the prior written permission of both the copyright owner and the publisher of this book.

A CIP catalogue record for this book is available from the British Library.

ISBN: 978 1 78125 424 0
eISBN: 978 1 78283 144 0

Text design by sue@lambledesign.demon.co.uk

Typeset in Helvetica by MacGuru Ltd
info@macguru.org.uk

Printed and bound in Britain by Clays, Bungay, Suffolk

All reasonable efforts have been made to obtain permission to reproduce copyright material. Any omissions or errors of attribution are unintentional and will be corrected in future printings following notification in writing to the publisher.

FSC
www.fsc.org
MIX
Paper from
responsible sources
FSC® C018072

SURREY LIBRARIES	
Askews & Holts	01-May-2015
658.45 ECO	£12.99

About the checklist series

Management can be a daunting task. Managers are expected to provide direction, foster commitment, facilitate change and achieve results through the efficient, creative and responsible deployment of people and other resources. On top of that, managers have to manage themselves and develop their own personal skills. Just keeping up is a challenge – and we cannot be experts in everything.

The checklists in this series have been developed over many years by the Chartered Management Institute (CMI) to meet this challenge by addressing the main issues that managers can expect to face during their career. Each checklist distils good practice from industry to provide a clear and straightforward overview of a specific topic or activity, and has been reviewed by CMI's Subject Matter Experts Panel to reflect new research and changes in working life.

The series is designed both for managers who need an introduction to unfamiliar topics, and for those who want to refresh their understanding of the salient points. In more specialised areas – for example, financial management – checklists can also enable the generalist manager to work more effectively with experts, or to delegate more effectively to a subordinate.

Why is the checklist format useful? Checklists provide a logical, structured framework to help professional managers deal with an increasingly complex workplace – they help shape our thoughts and save us from being confused by too much information. At the same time, checklists help us to make good use of what we already know. They help us to remember things and prevent us from forgetting something important. Thus, no matter how expert we may already be, using checklists can improve outcomes and give us the confidence to manage more effectively, and to get the job done.

About this book

This book aims to help managers develop and improve their communication skills. Communication has been called the lifeblood of any organisation and yet, time and again, reports show that organisations and managers are failing to communicate effectively with their employees and other stakeholders.

This collection of action-oriented checklists and summaries of the ideas of seminal management thinkers covers both interpersonal and organisational communications. Practical guidance is provided on the skills you will need as a manager, whether it's briefing your team, conducting an interview, making a presentation or writing a report. Attention is also given to the abilities managers need to communicate in today's global digital world, including how to handle email and social media and communicate virtually and cross-culturally.

Introductions to the organisational dimensions of communication are also provided, including topics such as internal communication, public relations and crisis communications.

Contents

Organisational communication

External communication

Introduction

We can all communicate, but can we do it well? Whatever we say and whatever we do (doing, of course, is a powerful form of communication), what does our audience hear and what does it witness? More important, how does it make them feel? Feelings trump action and action speaks louder than words. In an increasingly volatile, often ambiguous, environment, we are blessed with many different ways to communicate across many diverse cultures. With new ways emerging all the time, we need to understand which channels and which techniques to use for particular purposes. Rooted in the basics of communication skills – both verbal and written – this book will bring you up to date with contemporary communications methods. It will help you think about how to manage communication within and beyond your organisation and will provide you with practical advice on what to do – and what to avoid.

In over 30 years of helping companies to articulate their brand stories and supporting leaders to outline inspirationally their organisations' dreams and their own intentions, I have concluded that communicating skilfully is one of the most distinguishing features of a leader. Leaders, in addition to speaking and acting, know the value of listening, reading, observing, reflecting and processing all that they hear, see and sense.

So it is of little surprise that communication skills are highly valued by employers. In 2014 a survey of employers in the UK carried out by the Chartered Management Institute found communication was the No. 1 skill they looked for when recruiting new managers

(67% of respondents). Team-building skills and the ability to motivate others – both skills with a strong communication component – were ranked third and fourth respectively.[1] So, if you are applying for jobs or looking for a promotion with your current employer, you will almost certainly need to demonstrate good communication skills.

With managers at every level expected to lead, their most time-consuming activity is communication. How can you motivate others to act unless you are able to communicate your vision? How can you persuade people that what you propose is meaningful enough to participate?

Communication is management's priceless commodity, catalysing seamless operations and ensuring an organisation focuses its activities on what is core to its culture. On the one hand communication supports innovation, on the other it reinforces the way we do things around here. Good communication is key to improving the many relationships that exist between manager and manager, as well as between manager and team member. A passionate embrace of our dreams and plans, based on how powerfully we communicate them, drives the productivity of the enterprise. Externally, well-managed communication is important for sales and is at the heart of enduring, profitable customer relationships. Conversely, poor use of social media can severely damage or even kill your business.

Communication enhances all aspects of life, from the professional to the social and everything in between. Ineffective or misunderstood communications in our personal lives invariably give rise to difficulties, but we can usually beg for forgiveness. In our professional lives, the punitive glare of the media or the heightened expectations of our employees make forgiveness harder to earn. The results of poor communication may have much more serious consequences.

'The 21st century will belong to the storyteller,' predicted Rolf Jensen of the Copenhagen Institute for Future Studies in his book,

The Dream Society. Yet, individually and corporately, we continue to ignore the opportunities presented to us by our ability to tell stories, and to communicate clearly and powerfully what we do, why we do it and how we do it. In the context of the technologies now at their disposal and the participation that we crave as social animals, leaders and managers throughout the organisation need to focus with more rigour, discipline and creativity on how they communicate.

In short, communication matters. To succeed in your career you need to understand this important topic.

Richard Hytner

Richard Hytner is Deputy Chairman, Saatchi & Saatchi Worldwide, Adjunct Professor of Marketing, London Business School and author of Consiglieri: Leading from the Shadows *(Profile Books)*

Notes

1. Chartered Management Institute; Association of Business Schools; Quality Assurance Agency; *21st Century Leaders*, London, 2014, p.16.

Ensuring clear communication

All communication consists of three elements: the sender who originates the communication; the message that is being communicated; and one or more receivers of the message.

Communication occurs when one person speaks or writes a message, or uses non-verbal body language to convey a message, which is received by one or more people. True communication is not necessarily the message that the sender intended to send, or even the words that the sender used – it is the message that was understood by the receiver. Clear communication exists when the message received is the same as the message that the sender intended to send.

Clear communication is critical to business and personal success, but it is often fraught with difficulties. This checklist provides an introduction to the basic elements of the communication process and outlines some principles that will help readers improve their communication skills, both as the sender (the speaker or writer) and the receiver (the listener or reader) of messages.

Why is clear communication important?

Because it:

- improves efficiency in all activities
- reduces the frustration which arises from misunderstandings
- promotes clearer, more structured thinking
- involves putting oneself in another person's place; it leads

to enhanced understanding of other people and to more effective management of relationships. This does not mean that relationships are necessarily more harmonious, although this may be the case.

What are the issues?

Communicating clearly can be surprisingly hard work. It is comparatively easy to:

- speak before thinking
- shoot off a quick email without considering the impact it will have or the impression it may make on those who receive it
- use words and phrases which mean something to you but which may not be fully understood by others
- assume that the other person has the same background knowledge of the situation or issue as you do
- assume that the other person is from the same cultural background as yourself.

Why do communications go wrong?

Because:

- the message is not clear in the sender's mind
- the words of the message do not adequately express the thoughts in the sender's mind
- the words of the message are not consistent with non-verbal messages also being given out by the sender
- the receiver does not understand the words of the message
- assumptions or prejudices in the mind of the receiver may hinder the correct understanding of the message
- the receiver's cultural values make certain forms of communication offensive.

Action checklist for senders

1 Prepare your message

Make sure that the message is totally clear in your own mind. What are you trying to achieve? How will you know if you have achieved it? Try to identify any assumptions you are making (for instance, about the other person's cultural background, knowledge of, or attitude to, the subject). Look for any underlying prejudices affecting your view of the situation and the message you are trying to convey.

Think about your communication from the other person's perspective. Ask yourself:

- How will this affect X?
- What problems might it give X?
- How does this fit in with what I know of X's objectives?
- How does this fit in with what I know of X's prejudices, likes and dislikes?
- Does X have the necessary background knowledge to understand the message?
- Will X understand any jargon or technical terms?
- Is this the best time and place to be communicating with X?
- What is the best way to communicate with X – email, social-media network, telephone, or face-to-face meeting?

Anticipate X's likely reaction, but do not assume that this reaction is bound to occur or be misled by wishful thinking. If your message is complex, plan and structure it with care.

It is unrealistic to prepare consciously for every communication, but if your message is particularly important or is likely to be 'difficult', it is worth spending time on preparation. Consider seeking advice from a colleague. Ask someone to review drafts of any written communication, and discuss it with them. Organise a dry run of presentations, interviews or conversations.

If the content is confidential, use your manager or HR staff as a sounding board. Consider doing some cultural research if the person the message is being communicated to is from another country.

2 Choose your words carefully

Check your understanding of any words you are not sure about, or better still, avoid them. Misunderstood and misused words can be dangerous. For example, if you realise that you do not understand a word, you can ask for an explanation. But if you assume that 'continually' means 'constantly' or 'without stopping' and it is (correctly) intended to mean 'repeatedly', there is a problem. The message 'Evacuate the building when the fire alarm sounds continually' could become a recipe for chaos and disaster.

Remember the mnemonic KISS – keep it simple, stupid.

● Eliminate unnecessary words. Avoid gobbledegook and keep sentences short. Your aim is communication, not literary elegance. Here are a few examples:

  – 'although' not 'in spite of the fact that'
  – 'while' not 'during the period that'
  – 'soon' not 'in the not too distant future'
  – 'I think' not 'the data appears to indicate that'
  – use short words – polysyllables are cumbersome.

● Avoid jargon unless you are sure the other person will understand it. The most dangerous jargon consists of words used in a technical sense that have a slightly different everyday meaning, as they can easily be misunderstood – much management jargon falls into this category. Acronyms and abbreviations should also be avoided, or defined on the first occasion they are used. However, if you and the message receiver both understand the technical jargon, use it to make your communication more precise.

● Prefer positive phrases rather than negative ones – they are easier to understand as well as being more persuasive. For example,

'Please call me if' not ' Please do not hesitate to call me if'.
Double and triple negatives can obscure your meaning. 'There
is no doubt that his request will not be granted' – well, will it be
granted or not?

- Use concrete rather than abstract verbs and nouns. For example:
  - 'sandwich bar' or 'canteen' or 'coffee machine', not 'refreshment
    facilities'
  - 'tell' or 'write to', not 'inform'.

- Use active rather than passive verbs for simplicity and clarity. For
  example:
  - 'I think...' not' it is thought that...'
  - You requested...' not 'It was requested that...'

- Use 'I' language when you wish to give accurate, non-aggressive
  feedback or to handle a difficult situation. This is more accurate
  and conveys the meaning more fully.
  - 'I don't understand' rather than 'What do you mean?'
  - 'I felt let down' rather than 'You let me down.'
  - 'I particularly need the job done by the deadline because...' not
    'Don't miss the deadline.'
  - 'I support your decision' or 'I disagree, but I am prepared to go
    along with your decision' not 'It's your decision'.

Be careful to avoid language that may cause offence or be
construed as patronising or discriminatory in any way.

Ask questions to seek information or direct a conversation:

- **Open questions** encourage the other person to answer at
  some length, expressing their views and feelings. They are often
  introduced by 'what', 'why' or 'how' – for example, 'What do you
  think?' rather than 'Do you agree or not?'

- **Closed questions** should be used to elicit short, specific pieces
  of information, even just 'yes' or 'no'. They are ideal for clarifying
  a problem or situation. For example, 'When did that happen?' or
  'Have you told your manager?'

- **Reflective questions** can be used to bring underlying feelings and opinions into the open, or to check that you have understood the other person correctly.

● **Statements** such as 'I hope you were pleased with that solution' or 'You sound upset about it' can also be used to gauge feelings and opinions.

● **Leading questions** are those where the question suggests the answer you want or expect to receive, for example 'May we conclude that...?' These are less helpful than other types of question, as you cannot tell whether you received the answer you expected because it was correct or because of the way you asked it.

3 Reinforce your message

It has been suggested that in any face-to-face communication the words used make up only 10% of the message. It is certainly clear that body language – posture, facial expressions, gestures, tone of voice and non-verbal utterances such as grunts and sighs – play a significant role in communication. If your spoken words do not match your tone of voice or body language, the receiver is more likely to be influenced by these than by the verbal message. 'I agree' said with a clenched jaw, or 'What a great pity' spoken in a light, casual tone, convey the opposite message to the words.

When your message is not what people expect to hear, take particular care to match non-verbal communication with your words. Bear in mind that people often hear what they expect or want to hear.

To improve face-to face interactions, try to 'pace' the other person's voice and body language. Pacing is a delayed, understated matching of the other person's voice tempo and volume, body posture, gestures and facial expressions. This is a powerful tool for making communications more productive, and can reduce conflict, embarrassment and reserve. It does not mean you will invariably get your way, however. It may feel awkward at first, but it is a skill that improves rapidly with practice.

Remember the old training adage: first tell them what you are going to tell them; then tell them; then tell them what you have told them. Providing preliminary summaries for complex messages and recapping for all but the simplest or least important communications will increase understanding and retention of your messages.

When a spoken message is important, confirm it in writing so that it is documented.

Action checklist for receivers

1 Prepare

Try to put yourself in the sender's position. What are they likely to want to achieve? How important is it? However, do be careful with any assumptions, as they can frequently lead to misunderstanding.

2 Listen

The receiver has as much responsibility for the success of a communication as the sender. Poor listening is a common communication problem. Causes include:

- the mind wandering, because your brain can think at a much faster rate than people speak
- fatigue or stress
- focusing on how you will respond to the message rather than on what is actually being communicated
- thinking about other things, perhaps because of lack of interest
- preconceived ideas and assumptions about what the speaker will say
- hostility towards the speaker.

A simple mnemonic, LISTEN, can help:

- **L**ook interested. Maintaining eye contact with the speaker helps you to concentrate; an alert, interested expression will, believe it or not, actually make you feel more interested (in the same way that it is difficult to feel angry about something if you are smiling and laughing).

● Inquire with questions, to check your understanding. Do not make assumptions.

● Stay on target, using any slack thinking time to consider the implications of what the speaker is saying.

● Take notes, to help you concentrate and refresh your memory later.

● Evaluate the whole message, watching body language as well as hearing the words.

● Neutralise your feelings, acknowledging to yourself any prejudices you may have. Try pacing the speaker yourself.

3 Read

Important material should be read carefully, but it is not always possible to read everything we receive.

Some unimportant communications, such as junk mail, can be filtered out and left unread. Some written communications can be scanned rapidly (reading the first sentence of each paragraph is an effective way of scanning a document, as these are often 'signposts' to the contents of the paragraph).

It is not as easy to check your understanding of written communications by questioning the sender as it is for spoken communications, but it is just as important. Points listed above such as taking notes and neutralising your feelings are relevant to readers as well as to listeners.

As a manager you should avoid:

● underestimating the cost of poor communication, in terms of both money and relationships

● making assumptions without realising you are doing so or checking them with the other person.

Understanding non-verbal communication

Often referred to as body language, non-verbal communication is a way of conveying information to others through body posture, movements, gestures, touch, facial expressions, appearance and sounds. Non-verbal communication can be used to support the spoken word, or in place of it.

Non-verbal communication, or body language, is a powerful means of conveying information and articulating emotion without speaking. This is achieved through visual signs such as a gesture, posture or facial expressions. It can also be expressed through sounds such as sighs, grunts or laughter. Having an ability to correctly interpret such signs will greatly improve your knowledge of how others are feeling and what they are thinking in any situation. Indeed, body language frequently betrays how people truly feel, revealing concealed emotions and deceits simply by a look or movement that contradicts what is being verbalised. There are also occasions when it is not possible to speak to others out loud, but the silent language of the body can often convey a message just as clearly as the spoken word.

For a manager, understanding and accurately interpreting body language can be helpful in a range of situations, such as one-to-one informal discussions with colleagues, team meetings, presentations to senior management or prospective clients, difficult negotiations, or performance appraisals. It is a skill that has equal value whether you are the speaker or the listener. Gaining an insight into someone's inner thoughts and feelings greatly enhances your understanding of that person and your ability to communicate effectively with them. However, it is important to be careful when interpreting the non-verbal elements of communication. Movements and gestures can have multiple meanings, so take the context of the communication into account and weigh all aspects of it before jumping to conclusions that may be unwarranted.

As well as being able to understand the emotions of others, it is important to be mindful of how your own non-verbal communication affects their perception of you. This will enable you to tailor your verbal and non-verbal communications to the specific context. Furthermore, understanding body language will improve your ability to interact with employees, colleagues, peers and bosses and build good working relationships with them.

This checklist outlines different types of non-verbal communication and provides guidance on how, by interpreting them correctly, you use them to your advantage.

Action checklist

1 Observe the listener's posture to assess engagement

Observe the body position and posture of your audience to establish how engaged they are. If people's bodies are angled towards you, it suggests they are interested in what is being said. If they are leaning back or away from you, this could signify that they feel offended or threatened, or are not interested in what you are saying. Look at their posture: are they slumped forward with hunched shoulders in dejection and defeat, or are they leaning back with hands behind their head? The latter might suggest a state of relaxation and confidence or indicate that you are talking down to them. Tailor your communication in response to what you observe by setting the right tone and taking an approach that matches their mood. Techniques from neuro-linguistic programming (NLP) may be useful to help you manage an angry audience, or simply persuade someone to see your point of view in a measured and calm way.

Watch out for changes in posture during the course of a meeting or negotiation. These can provide a clue as to how things are progressing before the end of the session and give you an insight into whether you have won, or lost, your audience. Make use of this knowledge to prepare your response in readiness for the anticipated outcome.

2 Master the art of reading facial features

Facial expressions say a lot about what we are thinking and feeling. Wide eyes, raised eyebrows and a furrowed brow are non-verbal indicators of the listener's true feelings. Many facial expressions, such as a smile or a gritting of the teeth, are well known and easy to spot. However, learning to detect the subtleties of facial features can give you an advantage over an unpractised observer by enabling you to anticipate a reaction. Even a practised poker face can give the game away with the hint of a slight twitch, blink or pupil dilation. So perfect your powers of observation to gain this valuable insight and use it to your advantage.

Being able to read facial features when someone is sitting in close proximity to you is easier than when observing someone via a video link or online where subtle expressions can be lost. In such a situation, look for other non-verbal clues which are easier to detect such as a raised arm or voice. As well as facial expressions, other parts of the body can communicate feelings and emotions equally well. Arms, hands, fingers, legs and feet – the movement of each can tell us much. So you should observe the whole person to get the whole story.

3 Use gestures to good effect

Gestures such as waving a hand in greeting or giving a thumbs-up of approval can be used in place of speech. Such gestures are especially helpful if your audience is not in the immediate vicinity yet can still see you clearly. When adopting gestures as a means of greeting or communication, be mindful of whom you are communicating with. Gestures such as pointing, for example, may be offensive to some people, and others may be considered excessively informal by senior managers or older colleagues, but this can vary hugely from person to person. Be especially careful when communicating with an international audience who may interpret the meaning of your actions wrongly. Some common gestures can provide an insight into how people are feeling. Biting fingernails or lips suggests discomfort, stress or anxiety; drumming fingers on a table and foot tapping are indicative of boredom or irritation.

Gestures can reinforce what you are saying but can also undermine it. Fiddling with your hair or jewellery during a presentation or keeping your eyes downcast during negotiations suggests nervousness or a lack of confidence. This may distract the audience from what you are saying or undermine their confidence in your words. Repetitive gestures can become extremely irritating and are the non-verbal equivalent of repeating the same words or phrases over and over again. However, used in moderation, gestures can lend conviction and reinforce your words. Choose the gestures most appropriate for your purposes and employ them to good effect.

4 Interpret body movements big and small

Obvious or subtle, body movements are another means of silently communicating our response to something we have heard or seen. When conversing with another person, observe them for signs or movements that could provide an indication of how they are responding to you, whether it is tilting their head or restlessly shifting in a chair. As well as noticing obvious movements, look out for the smallest flickers of movement, such as a subtle change in someone's breathing or blinking pattern. If you are trying to gain someone's cooperation or agreement, an ability to detect such subtle nuances of behaviour will give you an idea as to how well, or otherwise, you are winning your audience over.

The speed of movements is also important when interpreting someone's body language. A slow and deliberate movement could signify relaxation and confidence, as opposed to a fast movement which is often indicative of anxiety, anger or excitement. Repeated movements can provide a clear impression of someone's feelings. For example, repeated rubbing of the forehead can signify anger and frustration. Repeated head nodding could indicate that you have gained wholehearted agreement, or it might cover the fact that someone fears to express disagreement. Sharpen your skills of observation by taking the time to look around you as you speak.

5 Think about the impression your own behaviour and habits create

Repeated patterns of behaviour make us predictable. This can create either a good or a bad impression, depending on the circumstances. For example, a person who is always on time will communicate their dependability and professionalism. However, conversely, if someone eats the same lunch every day, wears the same fragrance every day or drinks their coffee at the same time every day, these repeated patterns of behaviour may suggest that they are unadventurous, inflexible and averse to change.

It has often been said that actions speak louder than words, so consider how you act in front of others. Managers who repeatedly slam doors communicate not just that they are angry and frustrated but also that they are unable to control their emotions in a measured and mature manner. Such behaviour is unlikely to gain the respect of their colleagues. Examine your own behavioural patterns closely and consider what they tell people about you.

6 Be receptive to audio clues

Tone of voice is a crucial aspect of how meaning is expressed. The same words expressed in different tones can mean entirely different things. Is a statement being made ironically or seriously? Is someone making a joke or are they in earnest? Tone of voice will help you decide. Various tones of voice can also indicate hesitancy and uncertainty, reluctance, willingness, confidence or satisfaction.

There are also sounds that can betray how we truly feel about a given situation, whether they accompany an action or a visual expression. The throwing up of hands in despair accompanied by a deep sigh, dissatisfaction expressed by a tut and a roll of the eyes, or a gasp and a widening of the eyes in surprise: these all communicate the feelings and thoughts of the person performing the action without the need to express it in words. Emotions can be revealed by sound alone, which enables us to judge someone's mood without even being seated in the same room.

Tuning into the sounds of your workforce will give you a clue as to their level of satisfaction, enabling you to discern disquiet before feelings are vocalised and problems escalate. If you notice that someone continually yawns, sighs heavily or tuts, this may be a clear sign of boredom, frustration or dissatisfaction which they may not communicate to you verbally. Of course, yawning may just mean that they have not had enough sleep and sighing that they are preoccupied with a personal issue which is causing them stress. Someone who laughs, whistles or hums a lot is likely to be a happy and fulfilled colleague, but they may just be trying to make the time pass more quickly. The insights you gain by paying close attention to audio cues will help you to tailor your verbal communications and your actions in the most appropriate way.

Listening out for audio clues can also be helpful when addressing an audience. Their reaction to your discourse may be expressed through laughter and clapping, sighs and grunts, or even silence. Similarly, if you are in a negotiation and the other parties repeatedly cough or clear their throats, this may convey unease, suggesting that they are not happy with the way the discussions are going. But it may just be that they have colds.

7 Take care with any physical contact

If handled sensitively, physical contact communicates meaning without the need to vocalise it. For example, a hand on the forearm invites a confidence; a hearty slap on the back expresses congratulations; or an arm around the shoulders can be a gesture of comfort. Physical contact of this type can effectively communicate understanding between two people. But the person performing the act must be confident that this will be acceptable to the recipient. Physical contact can, however, be interpreted as invasive or even threatening. In professional and workplace contexts, it is particularly important to respect personal space and refrain from any overfamiliarity. Again, this is an area where conventions differ cross-culturally, so educate yourself on such differences if you work internationally or in a diverse team, so as to avoid causing unnecessary embarrassment or offence, or in extreme cases laying yourself open to accusations of bullying or harassment.

A handshake is a form of physical contact that is widely accepted in the workplace, especially in the West. You can judge a lot by the way people perform this greeting. When shaking hands with someone, observe how they respond. Do they step forward to invite this contact? Do they step back as soon as the handshake is over or lean in to encourage conversation? Is eye contact maintained or do they appear awkward shaking your hand? How long do they keep hold of your hand? How firm is their grip? A handshake can provide an instant insight of how someone feels about you. It can also reveal something of your personality through the degree of confidence, openness and engagement with which it is performed. Bear in mind, though, that in some cultures a bow or some other non-contact greeting will be preferred.

8 Watch your physical appearance

Whether we like it or not, physical appearance plays a significant part in the impression we make, especially when meeting someone for the first time. Clothes, hairstyle, jewellery, tattoos and piercings all make a particular impression before we even open our mouths. Consider what message you are communicating to others through your dress and physical appearance. At the same time, be wary of judging others solely on how they look. If the company you work for has a dress code, this may limit how much autonomy you have to personalise your style of dress and appearance; but even if it does not, you should always aim to appear businesslike and professional.

9 Think about what your workspace says about you

If you have a dedicated desk or workstation within the office environment, the way you manage your territory will communicate something of your personality and the way you work. A desk strewn with dirty coffee mugs or food wrappers sends an entirely different message about the owner than one that is spotlessly clean. Think about the impression you are creating and bear this in mind when introducing personal items such as trophies, family portraits, cuddly toys, humorous slogans and plants.

If you have a separate office from your team, try not to keep the door continuously closed. A closed door sends out a message to your colleagues that you are unsociable, unapproachable and wish to maintain your authority by distancing yourself from those who report to you. A manager who keeps the door open is encouraging interaction and engagement and helping to create an open and inclusive workplace.

10 Act on your observations

Being able to anticipate how someone may respond, or sense how someone is feeling, is a valuable skill that can make you a better communicator and a better listener. It is therefore imperative that you act upon your observations. Ignoring them could lead to a missed opportunity or a weakening of a relationship.

It is also crucial to use what you conclude from others' body language to tailor your own visual and audio clues. Are you presenting the right impression by the way you stand, sit, gesticulate, dress, and shake hands? Be mindful of using such powerful non-communication devices to convey the right message rather than a false one. Remember, we all have the unconscious tendency to mimic the body language of the person addressing us. By adopting an open, honest and calm demeanour from the outset you will help relax your listener and engage them in a positive way.

As a manager you should avoid:

- being overly familiar in gestures or physical contact
- creating the wrong impression through your appearance
- ignoring visual and aural clues
- underestimating the importance of body language as a means of communication.

Albert Mehrabian
Non-verbal communication

Introduction

Albert Mehrabian (b. 1939) believes that there are three core elements in the effective face-to-face communication of emotions or attitudes: non-verbal behaviour (facial expressions, for example); tone of voice; and the literal meaning of the spoken word. These three elements, he argues, account for how we convey our liking, or disliking, of another person. His particular focus is on the importance of such non-verbal 'clues' when they appear to conflict with the words used and/or the tone in which they are spoken. Mehrabian developed his early theories on this subject during the 1960s. Drawing on the findings of two experiments he conducted in 1967, he formulated the 7–38–55% communication rule.

Building upon his early discoveries, Mehrabian has gone on to develop numerous complex theories, ideas and measures over the past forty years, making a significant contribution to the discipline of psychology. During this period, he has written and researched extensively, continuing his interest in and commitment to the study of non-verbal communication. He has expanded his field of interest from non-verbal communication in relation to the expression of emotions and attitudes to its application in areas such as human response, temperament and traits, and the impact of the emotional workplace environment on performance, to name but a few. He has applied his findings to fields as diverse as marital relations, drug use and voter behaviour. Similarly, his research and theories have been adopted and applied by others in a variety of fields including consumer behaviour and marketing.

Life and career

Born in Iran in 1939, Mehrabian began his academic studies in the discipline of engineering. Receiving first a bachelor's and then a master's degree in engineering from the Massachusetts Institute of Technology (MIT), he completed his education with a PhD awarded by Clark University. In 1964 he took up a teaching and research post at the University of California, Los Angeles (UCLA) where he is currently Professor Emeritus of Psychology.

Entering the discipline of psychology from an engineering background proved to be advantageous. Schooled in a subject grounded in 'hard evidence' and testable theories, Mehrabian understood the importance of substantiating his theories and experiments with trusted formulas and measures. Consequently, he has spent much of his career developing scales to quantify and describe complex psychological data.

Key theories

The 7–38–55% communication rule

Mehrabian became interested in the role of non-verbal communication and its impact during face-to-face exchanges in the 1960s, when he developed the often used (and misunderstood) 7–38–55% rule. This was the culmination of two pioneering studies conducted in 1967. The first, in which Mehrabian teamed up with fellow researcher Morton Wiener, was entitled *Decoding of Inconsistent Communications*. The second, which built upon the conclusions from the first and was undertaken with Susan R Ferris, was entitled *Inference of Attitudes to Nonverbal Communication in Two Channels*.

What Mehrabian and Wiener sought to investigate was the impact of the spoken word and facial expressions on an individual's ability to discern liking in another person. In particular, they were keen to discover the impact of inconsistencies between the meaning conveyed by the spoken word and that expressed by non-verbal means. The study focused solely on the conveying of attitudes and emotions. To achieve their objective, the researchers asked a sample of seventeen women to listen to an audio recording of female voices repeatedly saying the word 'maybe' in different tones of voice. The tones used were meant to communicate 'liking', 'neutrality', or 'disliking'. At the same time, the subjects were shown three black-and-white photographs of three female faces each attempting to express one of the three emotional states (liking, neutrality, or disliking). As a result of this experiment, Mehrabian ascertained that the visual clues (facial expressions) gave a more accurate result than the audio clues by a ratio of 3:2.

Building on the findings of the first study, Mehrabian and his co-researcher Ferris pursued their interest in the expression of liking and disliking by looking at two different modes of communication: tone of voice and the spoken word. They attempted to discover which channel best communicated these emotions and what the implications for non-verbal communication might be.

To test their hypothesis, they gathered a sample of thirty undergraduate students from UCLA and asked them to listen to an audio recording of nine words. Three of the words spoken represented 'liking' (positive language); the next third represented 'neutrality' (neutral language); and the final third represented 'disliking' (negative language). Each word was spoken using a different tone of voice. The sample was divided into three groups. The first group was asked to ignore the meaning of the word and focus purely on tone; the second was asked to ignore the tone and focus solely on the word; and the third was asked to use both tone and word to discern the emotion the speaker was trying to convey. From their answers, it was concluded that tone of voice is a stronger indicator of emotion than the meaning of the word itself. Drawing on the combined findings of the two studies, Mehrabian formulated the 7–38–55% rule with the formula: total liking = 7% verbal liking + 38% vocal liking + 55% facial liking.

Mehrabian believes that the person receiving a communication trusts the element that most accurately reflects the communicator's true feelings towards them. From the two studies it would appear that more is conveyed by the non-verbal 'clues' than by the spoken word.

Criticisms and limitations

It is clear that these studies are limited, in both the validity of the findings and their practical application. Indeed, Mehrabian himself admits that his equation is only applicable in certain contexts, conceding that the findings could be applied only where no additional information was available about the relationship between the communicator and the recipient. Its application is also limited to cases when the communicator is expressing attitudes or emotions, and when body language and tone of voice contradict the meaning of the spoken word. Mehrabian did not intend his formula to be applied across all communication. Yet despite his own caveats, his research has been widely misused and misunderstood.

Other aspects of the studies are questionable. The fact that his sample consisted solely of female participants raises the question: would an all-male group have responded differently? The subjects were expected to make judgements based upon little more than an unseen female speaking into a tape recorder. Furthermore, the words spoken were limited to just nine different and unconnected words. The language was also restricted, weighted heavily to either negative or positive. And other types of body language such as posture or gesture were not taken into account or measured. If they had been, Mehrabian's conclusions might or might not have been affected.

It is therefore difficult to apply the 7–38–55% rule to mass communications when the speaker is attempting to convey a wide spectrum of emotions and attitudes through multiple words and complex language.

It is also worth considering that in today's world of electronic communication, where tone of voice and facial expressions are often lacking, Mehrabian's theory cannot be applied. If applied to a medium such as email, for example, it would imply that only 7% of any message conveyed would be understood by the recipient – something which we know to be untrue.

However, despite such limitations and the criticisms levelled at Mehrabian, he was instrumental in highlighting the crucial role of non-verbal communication in the expression of feelings and emotional states. His theory reminds us that where visual clues are lacking, close attention must be paid to the words used and the way they are expressed if we want the right message to be conveyed.

Models and scales

Mehrabian's theoretical works extend to a series of psychometric scales used to measure different emotions. In 1974 he co-created the PAD (pleasure, arousal, dominance) Emotional State model with James A Russell to measure and describe a series of differing emotional conditions. To achieve this, the PAD model consists of three scales:

- the pleasure–displeasure scale which measures how pleasant an emotion is
- the arousal–non arousal scale which measures intensity of emotion
- the dominance–submissiveness scale which measures the dominant nature of an emotion.

As well as being applied in the context of body language and communication, the PAD scale is also effective for measuring differences in individuals' temperaments. This makes it a useful tool for measuring consumer behaviour and responses to marketing and advertising campaigns, among other applications.

In perspective

Mehrabian's early theoretical works and experiments aid our understanding of the role non-verbal communication plays in the expression of feelings towards others. Yet the implications of his research extend far beyond this rather limited finding. Indeed, his findings have been used to articulate power, influence and social attractiveness, to name but a few. The social impact of his work is evident in *The Mehrabian Polling Snowball Effect*, in which he identified ways in which skewed polling data can influence voters.

Similarly, his emotional scales have a widespread application. His measures have been applied in the field of consumer behaviour to assess consumer reactions to products, services and different shopping environments. The scales are used in areas as diverse as assessing the emotional impact of a workplace environment, the effects of an advertisement on its recipients, or a reaction to a drug.

Additional applications of his research have led to the realisation that the choice of a name, whether for a child, a product or a business, influences how that person, product or organisation is perceived by others and the impression they gain of them. It is easy to see how valuable this research is, especially in commerce where first impressions are crucial in attracting and retaining customers.

Mehrabian's work has also focused on stress in the context of the working environment. His research has led to conclusions about the impact of emotional climate on employee morale and productivity. Indeed, his interest in human response and the importance of temperament, personality traits and emotional environments is in evidence throughout his studies, with conclusions that can be applied in many different contexts. His work on personal characteristics and traits has covered top performers such as elite athletes. He has developed numerous psychometric scales which have been used both nationally and internationally to help identify individuals with high levels of success, emotional intelligence, and good communication and social interaction skills.

It is evident that Mehrabian's work and research has been influential in many different disciplines and has made a significant contribution to the field of psychology. Despite facing criticisms along the way, his theories and models continue to be applied to great effect in many different arenas.

Facilitating

A facilitator is a person who takes a non-directive, supportive approach to help individuals and teams develop, learn and find their own solutions. This is done by creating the conditions for learning and constructive thought, and using skills such as listening, questioning, posing problems and reflecting meaning in a supportive way.

Effective facilitators can help to improve communication and develop consensus within teams and groups. They provide non-directive leadership and support to assist teams and groups in understanding common objectives, identifying problems and finding workable solutions.

Facilitation also provides support to individuals, with the aim of building their confidence and enabling them to improve their performance and increase the efficiency of the organisation as a whole. Employees who feel supported by an effective facilitator are likely to become more participative, responsible and autonomous.

An increased reliance on teams and groups within organisations has raised the profile and importance of facilitation, and global economic and social changes have created a growing need for managers and leaders to act as facilitators. A high level and variety of skills and knowledge are required, but managers will find that developing these will help them to be effective within their organisation and to get the results they desire.

A facilitating approach will reduce employee dependency,

empower individuals and increase staff involvement, enabling
work groups to be self-reliant and to function effectively and
independently. Facilitation can also help to mitigate the impact
of organisational politics and to manage partisan behaviour and
conflicts. It can only work well, however, within an appropriate
climate, where responsibility is reasonably devolved and a blame
culture is strongly discouraged.

Action checklist

1 Understand the role of the facilitator

Be clear about what facilitation should achieve. The facilitator's
role is to encourage others to talk, although in some cases the
facilitator needs to steer the conversation into positive territory
or towards desirable outcomes. A facilitator is there to influence
the group, not to dominate it, and to support the dynamics of
the group, not to dictate outcomes. The facilitator needs to tease
out the main aspects of an issue or problem and ensure that
any discussion or investigation has explored as many avenues
as possible, providing options that will help the group move
forward. This can be done by being conscious of team and group
dynamics and using a mix of questioning and listening.

2 Create an environment that suits your purpose

Start by creating the kind of atmosphere that will be most
conducive to what you need to achieve, whether the context is
a private interview or a group session, a formal meeting or an
informal gathering. The ambience should be comfortable, relaxing
and non-threatening. The best room layout is either cabaret style
for team-based interaction or a U-shape for larger groups.

At the start of each session remind participants of the ground
rules of behaviour (such as switching off mobile phones) and the
schedule, including the agreed comfort and coffee breaks. Stick to
the agreed schedule, ensuring that the breaks are not missed and
that the meeting finishes on time. Participants should be clear that

everyone has an equal right to speak, that all ideas are worthwhile and that speaking across others will not be tolerated. Make it clear what you will do and what you will not, and help the group to agree on an objective that can be achieved in the timescale available. One possibility is to ask participants to write their own ground rules on a flip chart or PowerPoint slide to be displayed during each session as a reminder and a point of reference.

3 Develop empathy

Empathetic behaviour involves being 'with' people in their subjective feelings, problems and experience, but keeping a part of yourself objective, so that you are able to offer support from a constructive perspective. Remain neutral, act as a mentor rather than a leader, and encourage others to take responsibility.

4 Facilitation skills

Many different skills feed into good facilitation, including influencing and negotiating skills. The facilitator also needs the ability to:

- plan effectively
- run meetings
- set objectives
- assess situations accurately
- diagnose problems
- give effective presentations summarising ideas and suggestions.

It is also important for facilitators to be able to recognise the potential of others and to have an understanding of learning styles and experiential learning.

5 Questioning skills

- **Open questions** help to get people talking and exploring the issues. Beginning with 'how?' or what?', for example, is usually helpful here.

● **Probing questions** and **link questions** encourage more in-depth investigation of the issues.

● **Comparative questions** give individuals the opportunity to make a choice.

● **Hypothetical questions** can encourage discursive responses and allow you, as the facilitator, to assess levels of reasoning.

Avoid **closed questions** that encourage simple 'yes' or 'no' answers, as well as **multiple** and **leading questions** that can cause confusion or lead to predetermined answers. Remember that facilitating is about enabling the participants to arrive at their own conclusions, so let the conversation flow freely, only intervening to guide it when necessary. Ideally, the conversation should be among delegates, not one-to-one with the facilitator.

The facilitator is a neutral party whose job is to foster the emergence and sharing of information in pursuit of the session objectives. The facilitator's questions should reflect this aim. Often the challenge is to help individuals express their ideas and knowledge clearly, and it can be useful to help them think through the details and/or consequences of what they propose.

6 Listening skills

The facilitator has the responsibility of producing a summary of the meeting and rolling up the discussion at the close. The techniques of active listening can help facilitators hear what was actually said as opposed to what they expected to hear:

● Contact – connect with the other person, full attention and eye contact

● Absorb – take in what is being said by the other person

● Reflect – feed back what the other person has said

● Confirm – elicit confirmation from the speaker that you have accurately reflected what they said.

Similarly, ensure that others in the room are also listening: 'One conversation at a time please.'

7 Observe

To understand what is happening, the facilitator needs to be able to observe individuals and groups or teams carefully. A good facilitator should be sensitive to body language and the non-verbal messages that may be given or received, checking these out when necessary. Read between the lines and look for unspoken messages, nuances and disconnects, where the spoken word does not match the body language. This may indicate that individuals are saying something they do not believe just to please other people. Intervene when appropriate to move the discussion forward.

Body language can often be helpful, but people may make false assumptions, judgements and misinterpretations based on non-verbal messages. In this case the facilitator needs a high level of emotional intelligence and awareness.

8 Paraphrase and restate

Paraphrasing and restating involve putting what is said into your own words and accurately reflecting it back. This shows that you are listening and understanding what is being communicated; it also helps others present to be clear about what has been said. Restatement goes beyond paraphrasing. It provides a preliminary interpretation of the situation. The purpose of restatement is to check meanings and what you believe might be happening with the individuals or the situation. Be careful to do this diplomatically, especially if the topic is being hotly debated from different angles. A good facilitator will provide a balanced interpretation and focus on facts rather than persuasive suggestions.

9 Know when to keep quiet

Maintaining silence demonstrates effective listening and gives an individual time to think. Be patient, maintain self-control and eye contact, and demonstrate interest. Encourage people to take their time when they need to think about what they want to say. Silence can also be used to provoke truths and honest responses, as most groups find it hard to sit in silence. If necessary, ask some brief further questions after the silence to make sure there is no confusion.

10 Seek consensus and agreement

Seek to reach consensus and commitment to an action or decision by allowing time for questions to be aired, issues to be discussed and conclusions formed. It is important to ensure that all members of a group have an equal chance to put forward their points of view, and that discussions are not dominated by a few individuals. You may want to consider using methods that do not allow particular individuals to dominate, such as using voting papers for decisions rather than a show of hands. Deal with disagreements and work towards a compromise when necessary. Do not be intimidated by difficult situations or people and be aware of groupthink – the answer may be as simple as suggesting a coffee break, or breaking into groups to consider an issue.

Facilitators need to be able to set objectives and keep people focused on the key issue(s) under discussion, drawing them back to the point if the conversation is sidetracked by minor or irrelevant issues. The facilitator may also need to encourage teams to generate ideas via brainstorming and other techniques.

11 Encourage a teamwork culture

Facilitation requires a strong awareness of individual differences. These may include areas such as cultural background, personality, ability, attitudes and how people behave in groups or teams. A teamwork culture should be encouraged to ensure that objectives are achieved, individuals are motivated and developed, and the team improves its performance. Open communication, team problem-solving and group decision-making will all contribute to a supportive climate for teams.

12 Summarise and provide feedback

Summarising helps to reinforce what has happened or what has been learned, and to clarify the actions to be followed up on. Where appropriate provide feedback that will encourage team members and reinforce effective behaviour, or help them to learn, develop and play a more effective role in group discussions.

As a manager you should avoid:

● taking a critical, unconstructive approach when giving feedback

● leading in a directive way, coercing group members, or contributing your own ideas

● taking control

● allowing a group to lose focus

● failing to keep an eye on the time

● assuming there is only one 'right' answer or only one way forward.

Networking

Networking involves establishing, developing and maintaining informal and formal business relationships with existing and potential colleagues, customers, clients, suppliers and others. It requires an awareness of the value of relationships to both oneself and others. Personal networks overlap: A and B may be in the same network, but each will have contacts in other networks.

Taking an organised and proactive approach to networking has many recognised benefits. It can help to improve and extend relationships, bring you into contact with potential customers and suppliers, and build links that will help you in your business and your career. Networking may give you access to important sources of information, or be a source of development opportunities, support and influence.

These benefits depend on the investment of your time and energy in attending events, keeping in touch with others and making contributions that interest them where possible. Many people are happy to get involved in networking as a natural part of their personal and working lives; but others find it challenging and need to put more conscious effort into developing their personal networking skills and extending the range of their contacts. Networks are not static – they can evolve, expand or shrink depending on the perceived needs and actions of the networker.

Networking is both an important technique to learn and a long-established and popular means of building and maintaining business relationships. There are three types of networks:

personal, professional and organisational. However, you may find it difficult to establish the boundaries between them, particularly online. This checklist focuses on personal and professional networking, especially face-to-face.

Action checklist

1 Choose a personal approach to networking

How will you go about networking? What style or approach suits you best? Consider these three styles:

- **Conscious networkers** have clear goals. They recognise what is missing in their networks and seek to identify those who will meet their needs, and make contact and develop relationships with them. The approach of conscious networkers is considered and systematic.

- **Open networkers** also take a considered approach, but often take a longer-term view, building networks with the future in mind. Their objectives may be less clear than those of conscious networkers, but they recognise those who may be useful in the future and cultivate relationships with them.

- **Intuitive networkers** are neither systematic nor considered in their approach. They enjoy mixing with people and do so as a matter of course. They may even be unaware of the extent of their range of contacts or of their potential value in a business context.

2 Prepare a brief profile of yourself and your business

Prepare a clear, short, introductory statement that describes you and/or your business. If this is longer than a few sentences, you may lose the listener's attention. Be prepared to adapt the statement to the person you are talking to – this will prevent it sounding too slick. Use humour if you feel people will be comfortable with it, as this can create a more relaxed atmosphere and encourage others to engage with you. Keep your statement brief; no one wants to listen to a long diatribe about how wonderful your business is. Let the facts speak for themselves. In some contexts, it can also be helpful to prepare a one- or two-minute presentation on your business.

3 Design your publicity material

Design your business card, and any other literature you produce, to project a professional and businesslike image of yourself and your business. Think about the colour, logo, layout and key messages that will attract attention and make it easier for people to remember you. A business card has two sides: consider listing your services on the reverse. The card must make clear what the nature of your business is. If it is an import/export business, carry bilingual or multilingual cards. This will show that you respect your foreign customers and suppliers and want to make it easier for them to network with you.

If you produce a brochure, make sure that it is written in plain English, free from jargon. Clear statements, with plenty of white space, are more effective than a cluttered layout with excessive use of colour. Communicate in a simple and straightforward manner that you care about your customers and aim to meet their needs, rather than making a high-pressure sales pitch.

4 Attend meetings and events

Exhibitions, trade fairs, seminars, workshops and events organised by chambers of commerce, local enterprise networks, business organisations or professional associations all offer opportunities for networking. Do not overload your diary by accepting every invitation. Think about the kind of people you want to meet and which events will give you the best chance of doing so.

5 Make the most of meetings and events

- Arrive in good time: this will give you the best chance of managing the event to your advantage.

- If there is an opportunity to display your brochures, set out a few for people to pick up.

- If name badges are available, wear one. Having your own can be useful, as event badges often use small print. Place your badge high on the right shoulder, so that people will see it easily when shaking hands with you.

- If there is a list of attendees, take a quick look through to identify people you are interested in meeting and look out for them during the event.

- Don't be afraid to walk up to a small group of people and introduce yourself, but don't monopolise the conversation – let others do the talking to begin with. This will enable you to learn about them, and their interests and concerns.

- This is also important when you are introduced to people. Encourage them to talk about their business and their future plans. This will help you decide how best to develop the relationship.

- If you find starting a conversation with someone difficult, and for many people this can be the main fear of networking, think about what you might have in common. You could ask about their travel arrangements: 'Did you have to come far today?' Or inquire whether they have attended this kind of event before: 'Have you attended a CMI event before?'

- Make a conscious effort to remember people's names. Listen out for their name and focus upon it using whichever memory technique works for you – repeating the name to yourself several times over, for example.

- Consider how much time you want to spend with each person. When moving on, offer your business card and suggest you might talk again later. Keep the business cards you receive in a different place from your own, or you may find yourself handing out someone else's card.

6 Consider joining a networking group

Professional associations, business clubs and local groups set up specifically for the purpose of networking offer many opportunities to meet new people and expand your network of contacts. Think about whether you wish to meet others in your profession or area of expertise, or to broaden your range of contacts. Decide what kind of group you wish to join. Some networking groups focus on referring potential clients and customers to each other; some give participants the opportunity to make brief presentations to the group or include short talks from invited speakers; others encourage members to mentor each other in developing their businesses. Consider, also, whether a national, regional or local group would be most beneficial. Take membership requirements and costs into account when deciding which group to join. It is normally possible to attend group meetings to assess their suitability before making a final decision. It is also worth bearing in mind that business clubs often offer training in networking skills.

7 Investigate online networking activities

Networking websites fall into two broad categories: business and personal. But the boundaries are becoming blurred because personal sites are often used for commercial advertising and brand-based networking, while the discussions on business sites range from the trivial to detailed professional issues. LinkedIn, many would say, has emerged as the main business-networking site. It offers opportunities to link to colleagues, colleagues of colleagues and a third layer of their colleagues, giving potential access to thousands of people. The site also hosts interest groups and discussion boards where you can not only network but also raise or answer questions about business issues.

Social-media sites such as LinkedIn and Facebook have large numbers of users, so they offer opportunities to connect with a wider range of people than face-to-face networking. Bear in mind, however, that the online networking scene changes rapidly. For example, MySpace, a formerly prominent social-networking site, is now in decline. Twitter's popularity makes it a good site to offer real-time commentary on business events, to identify opinion-formers and to make connections by following (and being followed by) others with similar interests or areas of expertise.

8 Build relationships

Keep in mind that networking is not primarily about selling but about establishing mutually beneficial relationships and building your reputation. For many, the most effective form of networking is to be helpful to others by offering advice, leads, suggestions and ideas. This may be just referring your contacts to someone else who is in a better position to help them. If you believe someone to be a potentially useful business contact, be prepared to give whatever help and assistance you can and consider suggesting a one-to-one meeting to find out more about each other's businesses and to discuss matters of mutual interest. This signals that you are interested in them for their own sake and are not just out to promote yourself and your business.

9 Listen to the contributions of others

Business presentations at meetings can be ideal for picking up possible leads: for example, people sometimes mention their problems in a group context, rather than confiding only in their business partners. You may also identify competitors who could benefit from a partnership arrangement.

10 Keep records

Set up a database of contacts and update it regularly. Although it is not good practice to take notes while talking to people, it may be possible to jot down a few key words which you can expand on later – after the event, but while your memory is still fresh.

Follow up on contacts as appropriate. Regular contact with people will increase the chances that they will remember you and steer business in your direction.

As a manager you should avoid:

- making promises you cannot keep – or breaking those you do make
- missing opportunities to be useful to others
- forgetting the names of contacts or failing to consider their needs
- retreating into a corner at business meetings
- only contacting people when you want something from them
- overloading your diary with networking events without considering which will be most useful
- confusing virtual networking with real-life networking – especially if the site allows you to cold-call strangers to make a connection.

Using social media effectively

Andreas Kaplan and Michael Heinlein define social media as: 'A group of internet-based applications … that allow the creation and exchange of user-generated content.'

Social media consist of a range of platforms and tools that allow anyone with internet access to connect and interact with others in a digital environment. They provide opportunities for individuals and organisations to share information and news, exchange views and opinions, offer advice and support, and collaborate on the creation, development and curation of content. Social media include online social-networking sites such as LinkedIn and Facebook, blogs and micro-blogs such as Twitter and Tumblr, online communities and virtual worlds such as Second Life, and more specialised content communities such as YouTube for video-based material and Pinterest for visual images.

The advent of social media has revolutionised the way we communicate, interact and engage with others, on both a personal and a professional level. Social media enable us to transcend boundaries, connecting and interacting with people we would have had no opportunity of meeting in the past. Advances in technology have resulted in increasingly sophisticated ways of engaging with others. Communicating via social media is not merely restricted to the written word: the development of visual and audio technologies means that messages can be conveyed with dynamism, increasing audience engagement and reinforcing what we have to say in an active and memorable fashion. Mobile technologies, such as smartphones, allow us to remain connected while on the move, away from home or the office. As such, we are never more than a tweet, blog post or link away from keeping in touch.

This level of connectivity offers myriad opportunities for us to develop our personal networks; enhance our personal reputations; engage in promoting products and services at relatively low cost compared with the expense of print or even online advertising; access, gather and share information; and keep abreast of current events and breaking news in our areas of interest and activity. But it is important to keep the pitfalls in mind: reputations which have taken years to build can be destroyed in a moment by a careless word or a malicious comment; and the volume of information and contacts open to us can become time-consuming, distracting and overwhelming. This checklist aims to provide an introduction to social media, as well as advice and guidance, for individuals wishing to explore the potential of social media for personal and/or professional advantage.

Action checklist

1 Establish your objectives

To get the most from social media, it is important to be clear about your reasons for using it. These may include:

- keeping in touch with friends and family
- making new friends or re-establishing previous acquaintances
- becoming part of a community of likeminded individuals with similar interests or aims
- giving and receiving advice and support
- influencing public opinion and campaigning on social or political issues
- engaging in self-promotion – building a reputation as an expert in your field
- promoting and gaining feedback on your products or services

- starting or expanding a network of professional contacts
- keeping up-to-date with news and developments in your field of interest
- gathering and sharing information
- carrying out research on a sector or market – identifying and making contact with key players
- finding out about consumer needs, wishes and preferences
- looking out for job and career opportunities – or potential recruits for your business.

It is also crucial to decide whether you intend to use social media for personal or professional purposes, as this will influence your choice of platform. Define the groups of people you want to influence, inform and interact with and the aims you wish to achieve, as this will help you to select the right platform to meet your needs. For example, many people use LinkedIn for professional networking and/or job hunting and Facebook for keeping in touch with family and friends. However, if Facebook users are a key market for your business, you may wish to have a presence there to find out about their views and preferences.

2 Identify your audience and the social-media platforms they use

Who do you want to reach? Friends and family, or business contacts and work colleagues? Some social-media platforms are intended principally for business/professional use; others are designed for more informal, personal use.

Consider the demographic you want to connect with and which platform will best enable you to fulfil this objective. Such things as age or location may point towards a particular platform. Think about whether you want to engage with people within a specific region, or if you want to extend your reach nationally or even internationally.

3 Evaluate a variety of social-media platforms

Whether you are looking for a 'bells and whistles' approach or a simple and easy means of communicating, assess what each type of social media has to offer. Time spent comparing platforms before making your decision will be worthwhile, as it will ensure that you choose those with the capacity and capability to meet your criteria and enable you to achieve your objectives. However, if you have little personal knowledge of social media, it can be helpful to consult someone in your organisation who is well informed and use their knowledge and experience. This could save you a lot of time.

Consider such things as:

- applications and add-ons
- interface/graphics
- level of customisation
- ease of set-up and/or use
- search functions
- ability to download video/audio content
- privacy settings
- alerts/notifications.

Bear in mind, too, that social media are rapidly evolving – sites that are hugely popular one year may be in decline the next. Monitor developments and check that the platforms you are using are still the best for your purposes. Look out for mentions of new platforms that are quickly gaining traction.

4 Consider the technical implications

When making your platform selection, take into account the technology required to support it. For example, telephones, smartphones, phone signals, connection speeds, broadband speeds and software could all influence your choice. If you do not have the appropriate technology in place, calculate the cost and time implications of acquiring it. Be aware that although the costs of investing in social media are easy to identify, the benefits will be difficult to measure in concrete terms.

5 Establish an online profile

Once you have made your selection, the next step is to sign up and create an online presence, providing personal details about yourself. Your profile is your public face online, enabling others to find you and decide whether you are someone worth connecting with. Think carefully about what information you wish to make publicly available online and the image of yourself that you are projecting.

At the same time, bear in mind that social-media platforms have thousands of subscribers. Try to create a profile that offers information that is sufficiently detailed and specific to enable others to find you easily, and distinctive enough to make you stand out from the crowd. If you have a common name, it may be helpful to include additional information such as your affiliation or location, so that people can trace you more readily. It may also be appropriate to include a previous surname to aid recognition.

A photograph is an effective means of identifying someone online and can help to create rapport. Your intended audience will determine whether a professional photograph or an informal holiday snap is appropriate. The image should be clear and current, especially in professional contexts. However, if you are hoping to re-engage with former acquaintances, consider whether a contemporary picture will identify you as the person they remember from the past. Keep your profile updated to reflect current interests, occupation, marital status, location, etc. For professional networks, include titles, qualifications, job history, experience and expertise in order to engage fellow professionals.

6 Build and manage your network

Whether for personal or professional gain, using social media is an excellent way to build strong networks of contacts. A diverse network of people can provide you with a lot of information and/ or be a solid source of support, and potentially open up new opportunities for you in your career or business. Actively seek out useful contacts by 'following' others, 'liking' and engaging with their postings, and sending them invitations to join your network, rather than expecting others to find you.

Review your contact list regularly and assess whether the relationships are still relevant and useful. Situations change so that you may no longer have much in common with certain contacts. Similarly, you may have been 'introduced' to someone or accepted an invitation that has proved not to be beneficial to either side. It can be more valuable to focus on a select group of useful contacts than to go for the highest possible number of contacts, whether or not they are relevant or helpful.

7 Gather and share information

Social media offer an effective means of gathering as well as sharing information and experiences. Learning about others' lives, interests and opinions can be beneficial – on both a personal and a professional level. Social media also give you access to a wealth of real-time news and opinion, which may not be available in formally published formats. It can be invaluable in keeping up-to-date with developments in your field of interest, getting a sense of existing and potential marketplaces, or gauging consumer opinion.

You may decide to use social media primarily as a means of learning about others as opposed to sharing information yourself. Bear in mind, however, that social media are all about interaction and reciprocity and be ready to give as well as receive. If you come across information you know will be of interest to others in your network, be prepared to share it. Responding to others' requests for information may be time-consuming, but it will enhance your reputation and you may well reap the rewards in the future.

8 Choose your words carefully

Although self-promotion may be your primary reason for using social media, refrain from sharing the minutiae of your daily life. Rather, populate your postings with interesting comments and information that will be of interest to your followers and contacts. Write clearly so that others can follow your thoughts easily without misinterpretation. Write succinctly, as lengthy discourse can be off-putting. On some platforms, such as Twitter, postings are limited to a set number of characters.

Think about what you intend to write before publishing it. Refrain from posting comments that you could later come to regret, such as a knee-jerk response to remarks you disagree with or believe to be inaccurate. Although a controversial comment can sometimes spark a good debate, rude, offensive or defamatory remarks should be avoided at all times.

Think carefully, too, before responding to criticism or allegations directed against you. It is important to engage with criticism and to correct misconceptions and misunderstandings. If you handle this in a reasonable and sensitive manner, without being defensive or aggressive, you should, in many cases, be able to contain or even gain advantage from the situation before it gets out of hand. In extreme cases you may wish to 'report' an abusive person to the relevant administrator or moderator, but this should be regarded as a last resort. The focus at all times should be on building rather than damaging personal relationships.

As well as what you write, think about the way you write, bearing in mind that the non-verbal, visual elements of communication are often lacking online and that this can lead to misunderstandings. Consider questions such as: Is the tone right? Is humour appropriate? Will my audience understand abbreviations? Spelling and grammar checks are important for communicating with a professional audience but may be less so for close family and friends.

Remember that you will be judged by what you say and how you say it, so make sure you pitch your postings at the right level and express yourself in the most appropriate way.

9 Reinforce your message

As well as considering your choice of words, decide whether your message could be better conveyed, or supported, by additional media such as photographs, videos and audio recordings. It may also be appropriate to post links to other sources of information. If so, it is good practice to write a short précis or an explanation of why you think the chosen link is particularly worth sharing. Engage your audience by making your communications interactive. Pose questions, start discussions and invite feedback, interspersing text, visuals and audio to help you achieve this goal. However, consider download times and speed restrictions, which may prevent some of your recipients from reading your message in its entirety, before posting large files.

10 Take privacy and security issues seriously

Think carefully about the level of detail or personal information you choose to disclose. Bear in mind that information you post online may be viewed by your employer or prospective employers, clients and customers, as well as personal contacts, friends and family. Most social-media sites give you the opportunity to decide what information is shared with whom; take the time to review security settings and update your preferences. As well as protecting your own privacy, it is important to respect the privacy of others, so do not share things that are not yours to share without getting prior permission, and make sure that your postings comply with the requirements of copyright legislation.

Be aware of the risks posed by malicious internet users such as hackers or distributors of computer viruses and of the possibility of identity theft, and take the necessary precautions. For example, keep your anti-virus software up-to-date; avoid using the same login details for every site; and make sure your passwords are secure.

11 Keep work and home life separate

Your choice of contacts may mean that there are links connecting your personal and professional lives. This can be problematical when deciding what to post, as well how to communicate your message. For example, do your business contacts need to know what you did at the weekend? Or will your friends be interested in an account of a recent conference you attended? It is sensible to keep these two areas distinct by using separate accounts. You may even see fit to use two entirely different social-media platforms to handle these two divergent aspects of your life.

The blurring of these boundaries may make it difficult to establish how much social networking should be done during work time. If you are an employee, consult in-house policies on the acceptable use of social media in the workplace, or in the absence of such a policy, discuss the boundaries surrounding its use with your line manager.

12 Allocate time to social media

To maintain audience interest, your content needs to be updated regularly so that it remains fresh and current. Make sure that you respond promptly to any questions, feedback (positive or negative) and open-ended commentary from recipients. Failure to do so could lead to audience disengagement, as contacts tire of waiting for your response. It could even affect your credibility with others if they interpret your tardiness as showing a loss of interest in or commitment to your contacts.

At the same time, however, be aware that updating can be a labour-intensive, time-consuming and, in some cases, an addictive endeavour. To keep on top of this and prevent social media taking over your life, consider setting aside a specific time of day, or certain days of the week, to focus on your postings. Resist the temptation to constantly check for messages and updates, as this may distract you from other important tasks and activities or turn into a chore. To avoid information overload, limit the number of alerts you receive. Check regularly for relevance and interest and unsubscribe as necessary. Again, designate a specific time for checking new content rather than endlessly logging on to get the latest news.

As a manager you should avoid:

- posting offensive or inappropriate content
- focusing on the minutiae of everyday life
- forgetting who your audience is
- producing lengthy, dull prose and failing to adapt your writing style to the online audience
- ignoring others' feedback and commentary on postings
- keeping too many superfluous contacts
- allowing social media to take up too much of your time.

Charlene Li
Social media and technologies

Introduction

Charlene Li is a thought leader on the use of social media and emerging technologies. She is the author of three influential business books and the founder of a consulting firm, Altimeter Group, advising businesses on the impact of disruptive social technologies on their strategies, organisational thinking and marketing efforts.

Life and career

Li was immersed in the internet from its early days of use as a business tool. After gaining an MBA from Harvard Business School in 1993, she developed an online advertising strategy for the *San Jose Mercury News* and then created the online publishing division of the Community Newspaper Company, putting 120 local newspapers online for the first time.

She joined Forrester Research, an international research and advisory company, in 1999, progressing to the role of vice-president and principal analyst by the time of her departure in 2008. Her research included search marketing, social networks, digital marketing, online recruitment and portals. It was there that she worked with Josh Bernoff, who was the co-author of her first book, *Groundswell: Winning in a World Transformed by Social Technologies*, which became a bestseller. The book focused on how businesses could respond to the challenge of more and more customers sharing information and opinions online. It received many accolades in business publishing, including the American Marketing Association Foundation's Berry-AMA Book Prize for best marketing book of 2009.

Her second book, *Open Leadership: How Social Technology Can Transform the Way You Lead*, built on some of the ideas from *Groundswell*, focusing on the leadership skills needed to manage emerging technologies by letting go of control but still avoiding chaos.

Key theories

Groundswell and the social technographics ladder

In *Groundswell*, published in 2008, Li aims to convince business people and organisations that they must acknowledge and engage with the fundamental shift in society that has occurred and introduce social-media technologies. Whether organisations deal directly with consumers or with other businesses, most of their customers and stakeholders will be online and will be sharing information about the people and organisations they encounter. To avoid being left at a serious disadvantage in the marketplace, organisations must engage with social media in a way that fits their objectives and their market.

In the book Li and Bernoff introduced the term 'social technographics'. Based on data from a survey tool used by Forrester Research, this is a method of classifying individuals and groups by their engagement with social technologies. It can be used by organisations to analyse the extent and nature of their market's participation in social media, building up a profile of each group or demographic that is important to them. Individuals may fall in to one or more of six overlapping categories depending on how they interact with content on social media:

- **Creators** make their own content, for example blog posts, audio and video.

- **Critics** respond to others' content and contribute to information sources, for example adding to a wiki, commenting on blogs or reviewing products.

- **Collectors** collate and organise information they find online, subscribing to RSS feeds and adding tags.

- **Joiners** maintain a presence online with profiles on social networks.

- **Spectators** observe others' activities online, consuming content without contributing to it.

- **Inactives** are connected to the internet but are non-participants in social media.

These form a 'ladder', with creators at the top and inactives at the bottom, and those in the middle engaging with social technologies in various different ways.

The authors stress that all organisations planning to engage with social media must be clear about their objectives. They relate possible objectives to existing business functions, so that the aims of listening, talking, energising, supporting and embracing are associated with research, marketing, sales, support and development respectively.

Open leadership in organisations

Open Leadership, published in 2010, builds on many of the ideas in *Groundswell*, focusing on the organisation and its own level of openness. As well as engaging with customers, leaders should also plan to be more open with their employees, the public and other stakeholders. More open leadership will improve efficiency, communication and decision-making in organisations. It can increase buy-in from stakeholders and help to solve problems collaboratively.

The book is built on the premise that leadership is still 'closed' in many organisations because senior managers fear the loss of control that will result from an increased level of openness. Li argues that new technologies mean that greater openness is inevitable, as well as delivering greater benefits than ever before. Again, the exploitation of new technologies will only be effective if the objectives are clear from the outset. Leaders should allow their objectives to determine how open the organisation should be and in what ways.

Openness, as defined by Li, involves ten elements in two categories: open information-sharing and open decision-making. Open information-sharing could revolve around six different functions: explaining, updating, conversing, participation or 'open mic', crowdsourcing and platforms (which set standards, including open architecture and open data access). Decision-making, meanwhile, can still be in any style: centralised, democratic, consensus, or distributed. Each of these will be reshaped by a move towards greater openness.

Each chapter in *Open Leadership* ends with an 'action plan', which translates the concepts in the chapter into practical tools for leaders to assess their levels of openness and to plan and orchestrate their strategies for increasing these levels. While recognising that the benefits can be hard to quantify, it does offer some tools for estimating the value of openness to organisations through increased learning, communication, support and innovation. The book also discusses how the mindset of leaders can help and hinder openness, how open leadership may be supported and nurtured, and the necessity of providing structures to enable openness while avoiding chaos. Li's final message is that any forward-thinking organisation must take risks. Failure is an essential and desirable part of this process, and without it, organisations will not learn how to make the most of new technologies and greater openness.

Developing a social business strategy

Persuading business leaders to think more strategically about their engagement with social media is the aim of Li's book *The Seven Success Factors of Social Business Strategy*, co-authored by Brian Solis and published in 2013. It is based on research on organisations carried out by Altimeter Group, Li's consultancy firm.

The main message is that as social technologies begin to mature, they should be a central part of any organisation's overall strategy rather than being viewed as just an experiment on the side.

The book offers a map for organisations to follow, arranged into seven key steps towards more effective use of social-media technologies. Organisations should:

- define business goals
- establish a long-term vision
- ensure executive alignment and support
- define the strategy road map
- establish governance and guidelines
- secure staff, resources and funding
- invest in technology platforms that evolve.

In perspective

Li's work has caught the attention of business people and technology-watchers, and an awareness and appreciation of her approach has been reflected across the blogosphere. As her work is comparatively recent, it could be argued that its true impact will become more apparent with a greater degree of hindsight. In keeping with the theme of her first book, *Groundswell*, online tools have allowed Li and her co-authors to continue to build on their printed works, for example updating the social technographics ladder with another category, conversationalists, to recognise the growing importance of Twitter.

Effective verbal communication with groups

For the purposes of this checklist, verbal communication is defined as voice-to-voice contact with all types of groups, whether face-to-face or through telecommunications systems such as telephones and videoconferencing equipment. Within an organisation, this may range from large staff gatherings to smaller team briefings, and from formal meetings to informal discussions between two or three colleagues from different departments. External groups may include suppliers, customers, business partners, competitors, the media and regulatory authorities. In each context, managers may play a slightly different role, but the principles of effective oral communication remain the same.

As organisations become less formally hierarchical, it is increasingly important for managers to get things done by involving and cooperating with others, rather than by simply passing instructions on to their team, other colleagues or external personnel. The ability to make things happen depends on adopting different roles, styles and techniques appropriate to the circumstances, and on being an effective member of different groups both within and outside the organisation. These can include virtual and international teams with differing skills and cultural identities. Verbal communication skills are crucial to being a good team member, whatever your job role, but managers in particular need the ability to communicate effectively with groups in order to manage their teams effectively.

This checklist provides an introduction to skills and techniques for oral communication with groups.

Action checklist

1 Define the purpose of the communication and the most appropriate communication method

First, clarify the purpose of the communication. Consider whether it is, for example, a meeting at which decisions need to be taken, a briefing session intended to impart information, or a brainstorming/mind-mapping session to generate new ideas. What is the communication designed to achieve?

Next, consider whether verbal group communication is the most appropriate form of communication or whether another medium, such as an email message or a written report, would be more suitable. Some tasks, such as sifting existing ideas, coming up with new ideas or involving people in a key decision, are best carried out in groups. Others are best left to individual or written communications, particularly where there is a need to impart large amounts of factual information.

It is also important to consider which communications method to use. Although teleconferencing and videoconferencing involve verbal communication, they may still have limitations in terms of the ability to read others because of time delays or reduced non-verbal signals. It may also be more difficult to ensure that all those involved get a chance to participate. An effective way to do this is to appoint a chair for the discussion.

2 Define the extent of the communication

Think about setting both a time limit (even for an informal encounter) and an agenda (even if it is an unwritten one). Be realistic about what you can expect to achieve within the group, given the roles and responsibilities of those present, and be sensitive to the pressures on other people's time.

However, open-ended conversations can be an important part of building relationships and influencing others. Be aware that participants may need further clarification or wish to put forward an alternative viewpoint, and do not be pedantic about sticking to the agenda and time schedule if others are happy to go with the flow of the discussion. If you have defined the purpose of the communication well, as suggested in point 1, this should make it clear when it is appropriate to close the session.

3 Ensure the right people are there

Group communication works best when all those present have a legitimate reason to be there, have something to contribute to the discussion, and have an interest in the outcome. If the right people are unable to attend, postpone discussions rather than waste time on an inconclusive debate.

Five has been recognised as the optimum number for effective debate and decision-making in most group discussions. This is because it makes it possible for members to adopt different roles, and allows a single member to be in the minority without experiencing undue pressure to conform. Getting the right people together, however, is always more important than getting the right number. If a larger group is unavoidable, consider using room layout to create no more than five subgroups and apply the same rules to each smaller group.

Discussion in larger groups should be chaired or led by an appropriate person. The task of the chair is to ensure that each member of the group contributes effectively, that different views are heard and that, as far as possible, the purpose of the communication – reaching a decision, for example – is achieved within the time allocated.

4 Prepare

If the communication is pre-planned, make the effort to prepare and know the subject in advance. 'Winging it' is a dangerous strategy, especially when others have had the chance to prepare. It can also be viewed as insulting to others who have taken the time to think things through beforehand.

Preparation does not just entail researching the subject. It also involves understanding the point of view of other participants.

Try to truly consider things from their perspective and consider their priorities and ideas on the matter in hand. It may be wise to have an informal conversation with individual group members beforehand to understand their viewpoint and highlight any potential difficulties.

If appropriate, send documentation out in advance, even if this is just a list of points for discussion. This will help others to prepare for the meeting and to contribute more effectively.

5 Facilitate introductions

If you are leading a group, introduce yourself and encourage others in the group to do the same. If they have not done so already themselves, make it clear what other people's roles are, why they are there and what they are expected to contribute. If expectations turn out to be unrealistic, allow people either to leave, or to suggest alternative group members.

As a member, define the contribution you expect to make and your authority for making it – whether your authority is personal (a function of your own position), for example, or vested (you have been asked to speak on behalf of someone else).

Set the tone for the language to be used. Will it be technical and specific, or more general? The language of communication must be inclusive to allow good communication. If possible, avoid jargon or technical language, particularly when addressing people from outside your organisation.

6 Be rational and respectful

Speak slowly, clearly and directly in short sentences. Structure your arguments logically. Think about what you are going to say, say it and then summarise what you have said. Link your comments to what others have already said, and clarify areas of support for, or disagreement with, the positions of others.

Most people respond to a logical argument, but verbal communication may be more effective if managers can present their arguments in a way that appeals to the communications preferences of other group members – for example, by using verbal imagery or making comparisons.

Take up a clear position on the issues, but be willing to listen to rational argument and be prepared to change your mind. If you do change your mind, explain why. Groups work effectively only if participants are open to new information and different points of view.

Mutual respect is crucial to effective group communication. When you believe someone is wrong, criticise the idea by all means, but not the person. Make any criticism constructive; for example, preface it with a word of support or agreement on a related topic. Resist any temptation to allocate blame; any attribution of blame for mistakes or failures is likely to lead to a breakdown in the group dynamics.

If you believe a group is taking the wrong decision, stay calm and do not become emotional in defence of your own point of view. Stress points of agreement and minimise areas of disagreement, with a view to finding a way forward. Reiterate the purpose of the meeting so that all members of the group are sure that they are working towards a common aim.

7 Be an active and considerate participant

If you have agreed to be part of a group, be active in it. Take full responsibility for its success or failure, be energetic and make positive contributions. At the same time, allow and encourage others to contribute to the discussion; listening well is as important as speaking well. If you have nothing to contribute yourself, admit it, and step down rather than waste the time of the other contributors.

Be aware that someone may be quiet because they hold a contrary viewpoint to others. Try to draw out their views without intimidating them, or allowing others to intimidate them. A contrary view may be the breath of fresh air that stimulates further productive discussion. Group members may be competing to present individual positions, so remember that you all need to cooperate to find an overall, acceptable solution which everyone will support and deliver.

8 Be aware of the dangers of unconscious domination

If leaders always give their views first, it is possible that others may:

- be unduly influenced from the start
- think that the ends are all sewn up and they do not need to contribute, just react
- get into the habit of not thinking for themselves.

Use open-ended questions that facilitate discussion, and make sure that you do not appear to be interrogating other group members. Give each member the opportunity to speak, even if you have doubts about the wisdom of their views. Do not put your own ideas ahead of the group's overriding objective.

9 Guard against a tendency towards groupthink

Groupthink is a natural psychological phenomenon linked to group dynamics which leads those within the group to conform with the opinions of the majority. Compromise may be necessary to reach a consensus, but groupthink can result in false assumptions and poor decision-making.

Reduce the influence of groupthink by defining your contribution in terms of how it meets the group's objectives. Then stick to your position unless you are genuinely convinced by the arguments of others. Have a genuinely open mind and employ listening skills throughout the conversation. Adopting De Bono's Six Thinking Hats approach may also help to prevent groupthink, as it encourages group members to adopt different viewpoints.

10 Make good use of non-verbal communication

Use gestures to reinforce your key messages and non-verbal signals to convey attitudes and expressions. Make regular eye contact with each member of the group and use non-threatening but positive body language to convey an impression of calm and confidence. Pay close attention to the non-verbal signals of others, as these will help you read the situation and the mood of participants: are you irritating or patronising them; are any opting out of the discussion; is one member of the group dominating others?

11 Bring the communication to a conclusion

Review what you were expecting to get out of the communication and whether you have achieved this. Agree a statement of decision and action. Write this up as soon as possible after the meeting. Make sure that all those present receive a copy, and send copies to any interested parties who were unable to be present. Be careful not to reopen the issue if a decision has been reached.

As a manager you should avoid:

- knowing too little about the reference points of other group members, and how their views of an issue may hinder the achievement of objectives

- allowing groupthink to lead group members to say only what they think the leader wants to hear

- dominating discussions and allowing your conviction of the merits of your own argument to blind you to the merits of the arguments of others

- allowing personal prejudices or assumptions, and consequent expectations of how particular group members will react, to affect you.

Team briefing

Team briefing is a process that involves managers and supervisors talking to their teams to exchange information and ideas. The basic principles are that it:

- is face-to-face
- takes place in small teams
- is led by the team leader
- happens regularly and is kept relevant and short, ideally no more than thirty minutes
- includes both organisational and team information
- offers an opportunity to voice concerns and suggestions that are taken seriously.

Team briefing originated in the 1960s when companies developed briefing groups which cascaded information through the organisation. Later the emphasis switched to the department or work group, and local information of relevance to the immediate group was added to organisational messages. The aim was to encourage the flow of information in all directions: down, up and sideways. It is important to view team briefing as part of a wider internal communication strategy, which is a process of ensuring that all employees are well informed and have opportunities for upward feedback.

Team briefing:

- ensures that everyone is well informed

- encourages empowerment, motivation and team spirit
- provides opportunities for upward feedback
- develops trust, cooperation and commitment
- helps people to understand change
- reduces misunderstandings
- reaffirms direction and guidance
- reinforces the role of the team leader.

Action checklist

1 Gain commitment across the organisation

Team briefing depends on managers' commitment to effective delivery and their ability to listen to suggestions and concerns. Line managers should explain organisational strategies and reasons for change with conviction and tailor communication to departmental or team contexts. They should also be open to listening to concerns and taking action to make sure that points raised are considered and a response provided. Gaining the commitment of the board and senior management – as well as getting them to contribute regularly to the core brief – will help to cascade strategic information to all teams.

2 Consult employee representatives

Involve trade union and other staff representatives from the beginning of the process. Discuss the purpose of team briefing and encourage them to participate in the design of the system. Reassure them that the intention is not to undermine their position or influence.

3 Coordinate briefings

The department responsible for internal communication should coordinate team briefing to ensure that messages and information are consistent, and to empower staff by collating their views

and passing feedback upwards. The internal communication
department should:

- plan and structure the system
- provide the core briefing pack
- develop communication training programmes for line managers
- collate feedback and ensure that it is considered by the senior
  management team.

4 Make sure that line managers are competent

Poor briefing and listening skills will undermine the process,
so make sure that line managers receive the training and
development they need to become effective communicators. The
emphasis in training sessions should be on the ability to present
with conviction; to express oneself clearly; to be consistent in
what is said; to facilitate conversations; to foster a culture of
openness where comments and suggestions can be made; and
to act on upward feedback.

5 Take care of logistical issues

Employees should be given the time they need to attend team
briefings. Remember that a willingness to cancel or postpone
briefings during exceptionally busy periods or when members
of staff are absent will be seen as a lack of commitment to the
process. Communicating is part of the day job, not something
you fit in when you can.

6 Ensure appropriate team-briefing schedules

The department responsible for internal communication sets
the process for team briefing. This is usually at least monthly
with a simple process for capturing the upward feedback
provided. Team briefings should be planned to fit in with wider
organisational meetings so that feedback can be captured in
a timely manner. This allows feedback to reach strategic-level
meetings and ensures that senior managers are better informed

and able to draw on information from different levels of the organisation when making strategic decisions.

7 Consider the content of the briefings

It has been suggested by Peter McCaffer, author of *The Higher Education Manager's Handbook: Effective Management and Leadership in Colleges and Universities*, that briefings should cover the five Ps: progress, policy, people, points for action and praise. The session should start with the core brief and a discussion of how it applies to the team, before going on to other departmental or team topics. This can help to keep the team feeling positive about the work to be done, the role they play in the organisation and the support they have in achieving their objectives.

8 Allow opportunities for discussion

Make sure that time is allowed for discussion during briefings. Any questions that cannot be answered on the spot must be responded to within a guaranteed period.

9 Monitor the system

The internal communication department should check that team briefings are being carried out across the whole organisation and that core information is understood. Ways of doing this include:

- manager walkabouts when a team briefing is taking place
- employee attitude surveys
- feedback forms
- audits by outside bodies.

As a manager you should avoid:

- confusing team briefing with other processes, particularly team meetings with different functions

- allowing briefing sessions to develop into lengthy problem-solving workshops or to be seen as an alternative to other team meetings
- imposing an off-the-shelf system without tailoring it to suit your organisation's specific needs
- launching team briefing without talking to the internal communication department
- assuming that only new information is appropriate or worth disseminating; frequently it is important to provide updates on earlier information.

Face-to-face communication for interviews and meetings

Face-to-face communication is a process of personal interaction during which messages (including ideas, opinions, information, feedback, instructions, feelings, and so on) are passed from one person to another. Within an organisation, face-to-face communication takes place in many different contexts and for many different reasons. It may be upwards, with your own boss or other senior staff; downwards, with junior staff who report to you or to other managers; or sideways, with colleagues. Externally, face-to-face communication covers a range of encounters, such as those with suppliers, clients or customers, competitors and industry peers.

The growing number of digital communication technologies and the increasing globalisation of business mean that face-to-face communication is no longer the only option open to managers for getting their messages across. In some contexts – the management of remote teams, for example – opportunities for face-to-face communication may be limited. Electronic communications by telephone, email and social-media platforms offer effective alternatives for many types of communication. Good face-to-face communication nonetheless remains a crucial skill that can make a substantial contribution to personal and organisational success. Clearly there are some situations that can be more easily and effectively managed face-to-face, and some would argue that there are advantages to face-to-face communication that cannot be fully replicated through the use of digital media.

A few well-chosen words can make the difference between a message that is rejected or misconstrued and one that is understood and achieves its purpose. Similarly, the time and place chosen for the delivery of a message, the approach taken or the tone of voice used, can have a powerful impact on the response it elicits. Remember that communication is in the ear of the receiver. It is, therefore, important to make sure that those you are addressing have understood the message you are communicating, and that you have understood what others are endeavouring to communicate to you.

Communication may be one-to-one, as at a performance appraisal interview between a line manager and a team member, or one-to-many, as at presentations and meetings. This checklist focuses principally on one-to-one communication. It provides pointers to the main factors affecting interpersonal communication in a range of organisational contexts and gives practical guidance to help managers to make their communications as effective as possible.

Action checklist

1 Consider whether face-to-face communication is needed

Decide whether you really need to give your message in person, face-to-face, or whether other methods could be just as effective and save you time. If it is simply a case of giving factual information, for example, and you know that the recipient will be clear about how to act on the information, an email may be the most time-efficient method. If, however, there is a need to discuss difficult or sensitive issues, a face-to-face meeting will be more appropriate. Consider, too, whether it would be helpful to forward information or documents to the person in question in advance, so that they have the time to review them and form a view on the matter before the meeting.

2 Clarify the purpose of the communication and its expected outcome

Think about what you expect to achieve from the encounter. Distinguish between your long-term goal (for example, to ensure that a major project is delivered on time and within budget) and the shorter-term goal of what you expect to achieve from this particular meeting. This will provide a benchmark against which to judge whether the communication was effective.

Practitioners of neuro-linguistic programming (NLP), which focuses on how beliefs and feelings influence our responses to language, ask themselves a set of questions before making a communication:

- What do I want to happen as a result of this interaction?
- How will I know whether this is starting/going to happen? What will I:

   a see the person doing?
   b hear them saying?
   c feel about the atmosphere?

3 Choose the time and place

Choose a time when the person you need to speak to will be able to give you their full attention. Do not raise an important matter that needs consideration when the other person is under pressure to meet a deadline or is expected at a meeting elsewhere. Consider the most appropriate setting for the meeting, the level of privacy required and the facilities you might need. If you are fixing a time and place in advance, make sure that both parties are happy with the arrangements. Be realistic and set a time limit within which you can reasonably expect to achieve your planned outcome. With open-ended communications, such as counselling interviews, discuss the timing with the interviewee first.

4 Prepare

Decide how much of the communication you can plan in advance. It is particularly helpful to do this when the desired outcome is known, is of critical importance and needs to be unambiguous. This includes, for example, contract meetings with clients or suppliers, disciplinary interviews with junior staff, and critical progress meetings with senior staff. Only take an unstructured approach where the purpose of the communication is to seek information or to counsel. In some cases, you may need to gather relevant information or put appropriate documentation together.

5 Consider your use of space

Respect the personal space of those with whom you are communicating and think about the physical distance which will be appropriate to the context: too close and you will be intimidating; too far away and you could appear threatening or distant and uninterested, depending on the context and the relationship you have with the person you are speaking to. Bear in mind, also, that this may vary depending on the cultural context. If you need to compete, negotiate or argue, you may wish to adopt an assertive stance, positioning yourself directly opposite the other person; but if you are seeking cooperation and collaboration, you may want to place yourself side by side with them. Think too about the layout of the room where the encounter or meeting is taking place and decide whether a formal or an informal setting will be more conducive to success. However, be wary of using your desk as an artificial barrier or to reinforce your status.

6 Ensure you are in the right role to achieve the outcome you want

Assume the role you need to secure your outcome, such as tutor, adviser, boss or salesperson. Do this consciously, and do not slip into another role during the meeting or allow yourself to be led into one. Make sure you select an appropriate role: do not attempt to discipline someone if you have assumed the role of friendly adviser. Only change roles if the outcome you are seeking changes during the meeting.

7 Greet the person appropriately

It is important to ensure that you have the attention of the person you wish to communicate with before you make your pitch. Tailor your greeting to the relationship you have with them. In some cases it may be helpful to establish rapport before addressing the matter in hand by smiling and asking how they are, but beware of appearing to be insincere or of beating about the bush instead of coming to the point. Depending on the situation, decide whether a businesslike approach or a more conversational tone will be appropriate. Be aware that some people may be nervous or inhibited, even if they appear at ease, especially if you are in a senior position.

8 Adopt the right tone

Use a tone that is appropriate to the role you need to play without appearing artificial. If you are seeking information, be relaxed, open and warm; if you are conducting a disciplinary interview, be firm and businesslike. Be wary of using the wrong tone or style, as this may send a confusing message to the listener.

9 Set the scene

Begin by quickly providing background to the issue to be discussed and summarising previous meetings or conversations. Ask for an update or new information and avoid second-guessing what the other person will say. Present your own case openly and do not be devious or clever. Aim to focus the minds of both parties on the factual issues before progressing to remedial action or a solution to a problem.

10 Be aware of attitudes, values and expectations

Face-to-face communication is heavily influenced by our beliefs and values, so try to be aware of the other person's viewpoint and take into account what you already know about their behaviour and approach. If you are aware of the results of any psychometric assessments, you can use this knowledge to plan and steer the interaction. Ask yourself how the other person views the issue and try to anticipate any barriers or difficulties that could prevent you achieving the desired outcome. For example, a person who you know is reserved in character, or who takes a factual, detail-driven approach, is unlikely to be comfortable or motivated to act if you present yourself in an overly extrovert and passionate style. Respect their values, but be wary of introducing prejudice by assuming that all employees in a certain group will view things in the same way.

11 Understand and manage the pressures both parties are under

Be aware of any concerns the other person might bring to the encounter that could block progress. For example, doubts about their competence to do a job, uncertainty about their career prospects, fears of what colleagues might think, or concerns that they may be asked to compromise on quality by rushing a job may underlie their responses. Recognise and face up to the pressures on yourself, such as the need to act fairly, legal requirements, deadlines and time pressures.

12 Develop your questioning and listening skills

Strike the right balance between asking open questions to elicit information, particularly at the beginning of an interview, and more specific questions to tie down the details. Use signals and gestures to reinforce your message and convey shades of attitude and expression.

Listen carefully to what the other person says. Be aware of their body language and non-verbal signals and use these as an indicator of whether your message is being understood and correctly interpreted. Listening in a focused way and reflecting back what you have heard will help to ensure that you have a full and clear understanding of what the other person is saying, and give you additional insights into their thoughts and feelings. Furthermore, the other person will feel valued, respected and understood and this will make it easier for them to be open and honest in their communication with you.

13 Bring the encounter to a close

Actively steer the encounter towards a conclusion. Use closed questions to check your understanding and assumptions. Identify the main points the other person has made and use their words to summarise the conclusions.

14 Stop once you have achieved the desired outcome

If you have set a clear objective for the meeting and achieved it, bring the meeting to a close. Do not dilute the impact of what you have said by going over it all again or straying on to another agenda. Being tightly focused on the outcome of a communication will save time and enhance effectiveness.

As a manager you should avoid:

● trying to address an important issue at a casual encounter when time is short

● setting an overambitious agenda for a face-to-face meeting – you will confuse the other person and finish without achieving any of your objectives

● adopting the wrong role or style for an encounter or allowing yourself to be led into one that is inappropriate

● forgetting that successful face-to-face conversation is as much about listening to the other person as it is about telling them things.

Handling effective meetings

A meeting is a gathering of people organised to serve a useful function; it is usually a face-to-face gathering of three or more individuals for a specific purpose at a specific time and place. Formal meetings, such as those covered here, are conducted by a chair person according to an agenda set in advance. Good meetings should have a clear objective, be attended only by the required participants, and be followed by the distribution of minutes with clear follow-up actions allocated to attendees.

This checklist does not deal with the legal requirements of company board meetings or annual general meetings. Much of the guidance given also applies to electronic meetings, although they are not specifically covered here.

Meetings are a significant part of everyday life, especially in the business world. They vary enormously in purpose, number of attendees, style, duration and level of representation, from heads of governments to members of staff within a small team or unit, for example. Meeting outcomes may have a national, regional or international impact, or may affect only the day-to-day internal operations of a small group or organisation.

Estimates of how much time managers spend in meetings vary, but it is common for them to complain that meetings take up far too much of their valuable time, which they could use more productively to do their jobs, lead their teams and achieve their objectives. Organising and conducting effective meetings that make the best use of the time of all those involved are among the most challenging aspects of a manager's role. A great deal of time can be saved – or wasted – in meetings.

Developments in digital communications, including telephone, video and computer conferencing, mean that, increasingly, meetings are taking place virtually as well as face-to-face. However, the general principles for holding successful and productive meetings outlined in this checklist are valid for all types of meetings.

To facilitate an effective meeting, managers need to consider the following elements:

- **Purpose.** What is the objective of the meeting?
- **Participants.** Whose participation is needed? If the right people are present, meetings can help to solve complex problems, build commitment and promote communication.
- **Process.** Once a meeting is under way, it often becomes apparent that it is not just about performance.

Effective meetings can:

- provide swift and productive communication between a number of people
- be a successful means of making decisions
- act as a vehicle for generating ideas and producing significant learning
- enhance the motivation and commitment of a team.

This checklist offers practical guidance for all those involved in planning and chairing meetings.

Action checklist before the meeting

1 Make sure that a meeting is justified

Meetings may not always be necessary or efficient, particularly those that are held regularly. It is important to make sure that a meeting is justified before committing the time, effort and other costs involved. If the information could be exchanged just as easily in another way, such as by email, intranet or online forum, a meeting is unnecessary. Ask yourself: Do I really need a meeting?

Consider the purpose of the meeting. Is it to:

- provide feedback or exchange information
- monitor progress on performance
- deal with specific problems
- brainstorm an issue
- develop future plans?

Can the meeting be carried out using technology such as videoconferencing?

2 Set clear, precise overall goals

The goals should be clearly communicated to all participants.

3 Keep creative and analytical discussions separate

Unless it is necessary to achieve the purpose of the meeting, creative and analytical discussions should be held separately. Creative meetings usually require a more relaxed timetable and atmosphere, and it can be difficult to switch from the routine to the creative and vice versa.

4 Decide who should be present

There should be neither too many nor too few participants, and you should invite only those who have a contribution to make.

5 Choose the date, time and place

Having a definite finish time aids concentration and may help to avoid time-consuming digressions. Make sure that the date and time are suitable for all intended participants. If a scheduled time cannot be agreed by all participants, however, consider whether you can run the meeting effectively without everyone present.

Waiting for a time that suits everyone can cause excessive delays and may dilute the purpose of the meeting.

6 Make administrative arrangements

These include:

- choosing and booking a suitable room, making sure that the venue is suitable for all needs – for example, check that disability access is provided

- making sure that the necessary equipment and supplies will be available

- arranging catering – make sure that dietary requirements are considered and met

- requesting secretarial help, including translation services if necessary, particularly if minutes are to be taken. The minute-taker needs to be skilled at listening and taking notes.

Consider using digital recording equipment. This will provide a permanent record that can be referred to if, at a later date, there is a dispute over anything agreed at the meeting.

7 Set the agenda

For each item clarify the objective and who will lead the discussion. On a full agenda construct a timetable indicating how long you expect to spend on each item. This gives participants an idea of which items are important and are for in-depth discussion, and which will be dealt with quickly. In general, however, avoid cramming too much into one agenda so that all items can be dealt with fully. Indicating whether agenda items are for decision, discussion or information also helps participants to come prepared.

8 Select the format of the meeting

Consider such things as the nature of the topic(s) to be discussed, the number of participants, the amount of time set aside and the goals you wish to achieve.

9 Notify all those involved as early as possible

The notification should include:

- full details of date, start and finish times and location
- list of invitees
- the agenda
- any briefing notes.

10 Complete your personal research, reading and other preparation

This may include making advance contact with any participants whose contributions may be critical to the success of the meeting.

Action checklist during the meeting

1 Arrive in good time

Make sure that you arrive well before the meeting is due to start.

2 Check the arrangements

Make sure that the equipment, seating, refreshments and so on are in order.

3 Welcome the participants

Greet participants on arrival, especially VIPs and any newcomers.

4 Start promptly

Clarify the objectives of the meeting at the outset.

5 Deal with administrative items

These include:

- introducing any newcomers, giving congratulations, thanks, good wishes and condolences as appropriate, and announcing apologies received from absentees

- domestic arrangements, including message-taking, car parking, smoking, catering, breaks and the expected finish time.

6 Despatch routine items quickly

Dealing with routine items quickly will allow sufficient time to discuss the important ones.

7 Introduce each agenda item

Emphasise the objectives and the expected outcomes.

8 Shape and control the discussion

- Encourage attendees who are shy or reluctant to participate without embarrassing them or putting them under excessive pressure.

- Restrain those who tend to dominate the discussion or are excessively verbose and opinionated.

- Allow only one discussion topic at a time.

- Keep different subjects separate.

- Balance contributions on contentious subjects.

- Keep control of time.

- Employ visual aids where they will help people to make their points.

- Do not express an opinion, unless this is needed at the end of the meeting.

- Summarise the discussion at intervals.

- Seek clear decisions at appropriate points.

- Agree actions and who is responsible for them.

- Suggest a majority vote or gain consensus as appropriate, where there are differences of opinion on key issues.

9 Conclude firmly and tidily

Restate the action points agreed. Fix a date and time for any
follow-up meetings and agree who will chair the next meeting.
Thank everyone for their contributions.

Action checklist after the meeting

1 Note the decisions taken

If they have not been minuted or recorded, make a note of the
decisions taken, the actions agreed, the people responsible for
them and the dates by which they should be completed.

2 Distribute the notes

The notes should be sent to all participants and to others as
appropriate.

3 Monitor progress

Check the progress of subsequent actions.

4 Assess meeting effectiveness

As with other activities, any assessment of effectiveness will
depend on having set clear objectives in advance, both for
the whole meeting and for individual agenda items. Common
measures of effectiveness include asking:

- Did all present contribute positively, in line with their roles?
- Was the discussion lively but good-tempered throughout?
- Were all relevant aspects of the subjects properly explored?
- Was consensus reached on all major decisions?
- Did the meeting cover the subjects within the time allotted?
- Did participants leave with clear knowledge of what had been
  achieved, and their responsibilities for future action?
- Were participants invited to complete a brief evaluation? This can

raise their awareness of their own weaknesses and help them to do better next time.

A sample evaluation form

To what extent ...	Poor				Good
Were the objectives clear?	1	2	3	4	5
Was the meeting well prepared?	1	2	3	4	5
Did it stick to the point?	1	2	3	4	5
Were vital matters covered?	1	2	3	4	5
Were clear decisions reached?	1	2	3	4	5
Was people's knowledge used?	1	2	3	4	5
Did people speak?	1	2	3	4	5
Did you feel involved?	1	2	3	4	5
Did you contribute?	1	2	3	4	5
Did the chair control the meeting?	1	2	3	4	5

As a manager you should avoid:

- arranging ineffective or unnecessary meetings which can waste time and money, exacerbate divisions, create bad feeling and produce poor decisions

- taking notes – as you need to focus on leading the meeting and contributing to it

- losing your temper

- allowing multiple conversations to run concurrently during the meeting

- allowing participants to get involved in purely personal disagreements

- talking too much or for too long

- insisting on having the last word

- being the first to speak, other than to introduce a topic

- allowing the meeting to overrun.

Effective communications: preparing presentations

For the purpose of this checklist, a presentation covers any talk to a group, whether formal or informal, from giving a team briefing to delivering a major speech. The same principles apply, although you need to tailor your presentation according to the audience and the context.

Presentations are increasingly common in the workplace as a means of conveying information or selling an idea or a product. Some relish the prospect of speaking in front of an audience, but for others the idea of speaking in public is terrifying. Whatever your natural tendencies, being adequately prepared is likely to make your presentation much more successful.

This checklist is intended for those tasked with making a presentation. It covers all the stages of preparation, from accepting the invitation to checking the venue. Most presentations involve the use of visual aids or computer software, but this checklist focuses on preparing both yourself and the content of your presentation, rather than providing extensive technical advice.

Many people nowadays begin their preparation for a presentation by creating slides in a computer programme such as Microsoft PowerPoint. However, this checklist suggests that it is important to think carefully about the context of the presentation and the message you want to convey before giving too much thought to any accompanying slides that you may wish to create.

Action checklist

1 Consider whether you are the best person for the job

Make sure that you obtain as much information as possible about the presentation before you start preparing. Find out how long you will be expected to speak for and the precise topics you will be expected to cover. If others will also be speaking, check what they will be covering, and how your presentation will fit in with theirs. Ask where the talk will be delivered and what equipment will be available.

If you have been given a choice, consider whether you are the right person to deliver the presentation. Ask yourself the following questions:

- Do I have enough time to prepare? (You may need to allow as much as an hour for every minute of delivery, especially if you are inexperienced.)
- Am I excited enough about the topic to transmit my enthusiasm successfully?
- Do I have the requisite knowledge and expertise in the subject matter?
- Would a joint presentation work better, perhaps with a colleague who has the right skills and experience?

You should be confident that you know the subject well enough to answer any potentially challenging questions that your audience may ask. If you have not been given a choice and you do not feel confident about the subject matter, take time to research the topic, try to adopt a positive approach to giving the presentation and resolve to do it to the best of your ability.

2 Research your audience

The most crucial component of a successful presentation is making sure that it is tailored to the audience. Whether or not they are current or prospective clients, view the audience as customers. Try to gauge their expectations. Do they want to be informed or challenged? How many people will be present? What is their level and background? Do they have any prior knowledge of the topic?

Knowing your audience enables you to pitch the presentation at the right level – not overwhelming them with too much confusing information on the one hand or talking down to them on the other.

3 Define the purpose of the presentation

Tailor the presentation to meet the needs and expectations of your audience. Think about why you are giving the presentation and whether the aim is to:

- persuade – this could be a sales pitch, or part of a discussion or consultation

- instruct or inform – in which case, you need to know your topic particularly well. Is this something completely new, or a new method of achieving a result?

- inspire – perhaps, for example, as part of a change programme or when reporting on the achievements of your team or organisation.

4 Assemble and organise your material

Assemble all the information you have that is relevant to the topic: facts, data, ideas, articles, quotes, anecdotes and references. Gather the material over time and organise it as you go along. Always keep in mind the purpose of your presentation, otherwise you could end up accumulating excessive or irrelevant information that will result in information overload.

Review your materials, and group items into themes and topics. Bear in mind that few people will remember presentations that cover more than four or five topics or sections. Are there metaphors or analogies which keep appearing? These could be used as a thread running through the presentation to give it a strong narrative focus or common theme. If you are presenting new information, try to relate it to areas with which your audience is already familiar. The audience will find examples and real-life scenarios easier to remember than abstract ideas or theories.

5 Prepare a presentation plan

Speech writing is a specialist area which needs thought and attention. The emphasis needs to be on developing a story or argument with key points that you will feel comfortable delivering. Identify the points you wish to communicate and structure the materials into a rough plan, aiming to include a beginning, a middle and an end. Start the plan with an explanation or reminder of the purpose of the talk. If the information you are presenting is complex, giving short summaries at the end of each topic or section will help your audience to keep track. Conclude the presentation with an overall summary which emphasises the key points you have made, and try to end on a high.

6 Write a rough draft

Use your plan as the basis of a first draft. Write freely without worrying unduly about the details – you can always edit the text later. Focus on delivering your key messages and on moving through the presentation in a logical manner. Outline what you are going to say, say it, and end by summarising what you have said. If appropriate, you may wish to adopt a storytelling style to present the information to your audience. This is an increasingly common and successful way of presenting, but it may not be suitable for all presentations, such as short ones intended to give people some basic information.

Attention spans vary according to the person and the circumstances; but most people's minds will start to wander after twenty minutes, however engaging your presentation and its subject. So keep it short. Present only the essential information and try not to exceed five key points. If necessary, you can supply additional details in a handout or direct your audience where to find out more. In some cases, it may be appropriate to distribute the handout in advance, as this allows people to familiarise themselves with background information beforehand. However, avoid giving notes out at the beginning of the presentation, as your audience will probably start reading them and will be distracted from what you have to say.

Some of the most effective presentations use humour to engage the audience and retain their interest, but in some cases this may be inappropriate. Bear in mind also that humour can be subjective. Do not try to incorporate humour for the sake of it; if you do not have anything funny to say, it is better to avoid humour altogether rather than embarrass yourself and your audience.

7 Edit and refine the draft

Review your first draft the following day. Check that the structure is clear and logical. Consider whether you can make the text more concrete, simple and illustrative. Eliminate non-essential ideas and words, and shorten sentences. Use anecdotes to enliven the text. Always keep the purpose of the presentation in mind. If something is not relevant to your purpose, leave it out. Decide how many facts and figures to include and whether the details are appropriate. Eliminate jargon unless you are certain that your audience will understand it; if you cannot avoid the use of specialised vocabulary, be sure to give clear explanations of the terms used.

Run through the draft several times, preferably in front of someone who can give feedback on content, style and delivery. This will enable you to make sure the timing is right – speaking to an audience should be slower and more deliberate than talking to a friend.

Time your presentation, as it may require lengthening or shortening. Ask your listener not to interrupt but to make notes, and invite them to give constructive feedback when the presentation ends.

8 Select appropriate presentation aids

A broad range of presentation aids can be obtained or created, using computer software and applications. Visual aids should add value to the presentation by reinforcing or summarising what you are saying. They should be:

● integrated – relevant to the topic and theme

- appropriate – to the style of the presentation and to the audience
- professional – clear, readable and consistent
- simple – clearly visible and understandable from the back of the room
- visual, as far as possible. Images, symbols, charts and graphs, for example, can focus attention on key messages.

When displaying text on screen, remember that 'less is more'. Keep text to a minimum and limit yourself to key words and phrases. If the audience has to concentrate on reading from the screen, they will pay less attention to you and what you have to say.

Where possible, choose images to minimise what is presented in text. This will help you present your material rather than just read it out. Images can also be used to engage the audience and help them to remember the key points. Pictures are particularly helpful to those who are visually oriented. Avoid 'death by PowerPoint'; instead, limit yourself to just a few slides highlighting the key points.

Be aware of the copyright implications of downloading images from the internet. Some copyright owners make images available for downloading and sharing on certain conditions through a Creative Commons licence. Make sure that you acknowledge the source of any images or graphics you use.

It can be useful to hand out relevant objects before or at the start of the presentation. Be careful when adopting this tactic, however. You need to make sure it ties in with what you are aiming to communicate rather than creating a distraction.

9   Start learning (some of) your talk

Adequate preparation time is essential, especially if you want to memorise your talk. An alternative is to create cue cards and use these as prompts. Both these options can work, but make sure you strike the right balance between being thoroughly prepared and sounding fresh and spontaneous. Whichever method you choose, it is crucial to have the outline of your talk clear in your mind so that you are able to maintain a sense of direction and momentum.

If you decide to prepare a series of cues or prompts, go through the draft and highlight key words and phrases. These will form the backbone of your script and your visual aids. Practise using the prompts and memorise the thoughts related to each of them. Once you are confident, transfer the prompts to numbered cards. Continue practising and reducing the number of key words required to prompt your memory.

Even if you opt for cue cards, try to learn the first and last sixty seconds of the presentation by heart. This will make starting and ending the presentation much more comfortable and help to put you at your ease.

10 Consider how the slides will be used after the presentation

In some instances you will also need to think about whether and how the slides you create will be used after the presentation. For example, they may be displayed on the company intranet or emailed round, so that those at the meeting can access the information. In such cases, you may want to include further information in a notes field or as a separate document, so that those who were unable to attend can understand the presentation. Add your contact details to the final slide so that people can get in touch if they have any questions.

11 Rehearse

Practice is the key to a confident presentation, so take every opportunity to rehearse, in your head, in front of a mirror, in front of someone else – you could even record yourself. Seek critical appraisal, and note any mannerisms you need to correct, or things you need to remind yourself about – to smile as you talk, for example, or make eye contact with your audience and keep your hands out of your pockets. (You could keep a list of these on a cue card as a reminder when you give the presentation.)

Timing is important to ensure that you present all the necessary information without losing the attention of your audience. Keep to time and do not overrun.

12 Check the venue

If possible, arrive well before the start to check the equipment and familiarise yourself with using it, sitting or standing in the place from which you will be presenting. Make sure that all visuals are clearly discernible from the back of the room. If you are using an electronic pointer, microphone or projector, remember to check these are all in working order, and that you know how to operate them. At the same time, make sure you have a plan B should there be any technical problems such as a power failure.

As a manager you should avoid:

- attempting to present everything known about the topic in one session

- arriving late – make time to relax, and get used to the equipment and premises

- using humour without due care and attention – make sure it is appropriate for the audience

- using material or visuals that, however good, contribute little to the key points.

Effective communications: delivering presentations

For the purpose of this checklist, a presentation covers any talk to a group, whether formal or informal. From giving a team briefing to delivering a major speech, the same principles apply.

All managers will be called upon to give presentations of some kind at some point in their careers. It may be an informal team briefing, a formal business presentation, or a public speech; it may involve updating colleagues on current progress or future plans, making the case for a new purchase or acquisition, highlighting the potential of a new business opportunity, or making a sales pitch.

Making a presentation or even giving a briefing can be something that managers approach with trepidation or even anxiety. Not everyone is a natural presenter, but the skills of presenting can be learned and developed over time. Making the effort to acquire and develop the ability to put your message across clearly and succinctly, engage the audience and make a convincing case for your proposal will reap dividends, in terms of both enhancing team and organisational performance and your own professional standing and reputation.

Careful preparation and practice are essential and will help you communicate effectively with your colleagues, clients and customers. This checklist concentrates on the delivery of the presentation and provides practical guidance and advice for presenters. The key points are to be clear about why you are giving the presentation, the audience you need to reach and the objectives you aim to achieve.

Action checklist

1 Adopt the right style

The type of audience, the expectations they have and the purpose of the presentation will determine the style you adopt. The size of the audience is also important, so try to ascertain beforehand, as precisely as you can, how many people are likely to be in the audience. Bear in mind that what one presenter sees as a large audience may seem small to another and vice versa.

For five to ten people, aim for an informal style with a few visual aids. The main consideration is to position yourself as you feel most comfortable – you may wish to sit or to balance on the edge of a table or desk, for example. Aim to engage all those present and to establish relationships from the outset.

For ten to thirty people, a more formal style will be needed, but it is still possible to establish a good relationship with the audience. Stand in front of the audience and plan to use visual aids as appropriate.

For an audience of thirty to a hundred, you will need good presentation aids and a formal style. It will be difficult to engage with individuals.

If your audience numbers over a hundred, view this as a theatre-style presentation: you will be on stage and performing with a microphone. Your facial gestures and body language will need to be exaggerated to be effective.

2 Check the venue

Do a last-minute check on equipment. Is there a lectern? Do you know how to use the microphone and/or the projector? Are your visual aids working and can they be seen clearly by everyone? Check who will be introducing you and when this will be. Make sure that water is to hand in case you need to alleviate a dry mouth, gain thinking time or regroup. Maybe you need to warm up your voice.

3 Consider room layout

If possible, make sure that the room layout is conducive to the purpose of the presentation. If you wish to promote interaction and engagement, small tables for subgroups of three to five can help to encourage participation when, for example, an exercise or task has been prepared. If you wish to avoid interaction, theatre style is most likely to be successful.

4 Check your appearance

Make sure that your physical appearance does not detract from your message. Presenters are usually expected to dress neatly and conservatively, but this can vary according to the culture of the organisation and the expectations of the audience.

5 Control your nerves

It is easy to fall prey to nerves when making an important presentation. A degree of nervous anticipation can be positive, as it can get the adrenalin flowing and help you to perform well. But panic can cause unwelcome physical reactions such as sweatiness, trembling, a dry mouth, or a blank mind. Public speakers use a range of methods to calm their nerves, from breathing exercises to visualisation techniques. It is worth trying some of these to find out what works for you. It may be as simple as taking a moment to pause, take a deep breath and adopt a confident, upright stance.

6 Establish your presence

Once you have been introduced, take a moment to focus on the audience; make eye contact and acknowledge their presence. It may be appropriate to start with some courtesies or pleasantries, depending on the context. Be positive. Remind yourself that you have something interesting and worthwhile to communicate. Do not forget to smile.

Explain why you are there and what gives you the authority to speak. Confirm the audience's expectations by reminding them

what the purpose of the presentation is and what you will be
talking about. Resolve any confusion or queries immediately:
it is possible you are in the wrong place or have been given an
inaccurate brief by the organisers.

7 Involve your audience

Attract the attention of the audience from the start by using
a visual aid or introducing something unexpected. Ask a
question, even if it is a rhetorical one. Say something that shows
you understand their concerns or expectations. Stimulate
their interest. Focusing on the audience can help to move
attention away from yourself and ease any stage-fright you
are experiencing. Asking questions and using visual aids can
promote audience engagement as opposed to just passive
listening.

8 Let your personality show

Remember that people are influenced by a combination of facts
and emotions. Put genuine conviction into what you are saying
and allow your emotion to show through. If you appear to care
about and believe in what you are saying, it is more likely that you
will engage the interest of the audience. Enthusiasm is infectious
and can be the most engaging aspect of a presentation.

9 Use positive body language

Remember to stand up straight. Do not lean on the lectern, play
with your hair, or fiddle with your tie, jewellery or clothing. If you
are more at ease on the move, walk around in a natural way and
use your hands for emphasis as you would in conversation. Try to
use normal facial expressions and, where appropriate, smile.

10 Take control of your voice

Project your voice by standing up straight and breathing deeply.
Adapt your voice projection and volume to the purpose of your
presentation. It is essential to speak clearly and more slowly than

usual. Speak naturally, but lower the pitch of your voice if you are nervous to avoid becoming shrill. Be aware of your speech mannerisms and consciously avoid repeating them. Avoid hesitating: if you have lost your place or your nerve, just pause, but try not to say 'um' or 'er'. Common fears are that you will dry up or finish too soon – good preparation can help to avoid both. Typically, presenters find they have too much content, rather than too little.

11 Introduce variety

Vary the timing of your delivery and the pitch of your voice. Speed up or slow down and change tone in different sections of the talk. Use inflections and emphases even if you think they sound exaggerated. Pause occasionally or stop completely in a long presentation – the audience needs time to absorb the content and you need time to reflect. Are you going too quickly? Have you put your hands in your pockets without realising it?

12 Build rapport with the audience

Maintain eye contact and play to people you know or sense to be sympathetic. Demonstrate the relevance of your presentation to them and avoid using 'I' or 'me' too often. Beware of fixing your eyes on a single person or even a small number of people in the audience, as those in question may find this uncomfortable and others may feel excluded.

13 Use visual aids and technology appropriately

Visual aids and illustrations can reinforce your message, highlight the key points and increase the impact of your presentation. But keep it simple and avoid overdoing it. Too many images can distract from what you are saying. People will be unable to take in the implications of large tables of data, so try to pinpoint the key facts they need to understand. If you are using presentation software, do not fill your slides with excessive amounts of text from your script. The audience will end up giving more attention to reading the text than listening to your voice.

14 Introduce humour

In the right context and if you are confident and have the natural style to pull it off, humour can lighten or vary the mood. Only use humour to support the subject of the presentation, not for its own sake. Beware of making remarks that could cause offence or be perceived as unkind to or derogatory of anyone present. Bad jokes are a poor use of humour and may fall flat, undermining your position and increasing the pressure on you.

15 Manage the unexpected

Come to terms with the fact that you will occasionally make mistakes, and that disturbances and distractions will occur. What matters is not that they happen, but how you handle them. Acknowledge rather than ignore interruptions and try to deflect or make light of them through the use of humour. Most people will be generally sympathetic and supportive – they may well have been in the same position themselves.

16 Take care with improvisation

Thorough preparation is essential, but you may engage the trust and attention of the audience better if your presentation does not come over as overly slick or glib. Remember to adjust to mood and atmosphere. A certain amount of improvisation can be helpful, but be careful not to be led off-track, as this will detract from the message you want to communicate.

17 Bring your presentation to a clear conclusion

Draw your presentation to a timely conclusion. Be brief and summarise your position or recommendations, but do not repeat the whole argument or focus on the details. Try to end on a positive note in terms of energy, tone and content. It is better to leave the audience wanting slightly more, rather than to ramble on once you have made your point.

18 Take a positive approach to questions

Actively encourage questions appropriate to the purpose and context of the presentation. Repeat each question you take, in case people have not heard it clearly and are confused by your response. If you do not know the answer, do not be afraid of admitting it; offer to find out and come back to the person concerned later. Avoid getting drawn into debates or arguments.

As a manager you should avoid:

- trying to cover too much in one presentation – this can confuse rather than help your audience; it may also create time pressures that lead you to rush through your presentation, speaking too fast for people to keep up with what you are saying

- overcomplicating the room layout – try to create an environment in which the audience will feel comfortable

- using humour without due care and attention – humour can lighten the mood, but used inappropriately, it may turn the audience against you.

Effective negotiation

Negotiation is a mutual discussion with the aim of resolving a difference of opinion or a dispute, or of settling the terms of an agreement or transaction.

This checklist introduces techniques that can improve the success of negotiations in the business environment.

Negotiation takes place whenever two or more people or groups desire outcomes which are interdependent. Successful negotiating results in a win–win agreement in which all parties gain overall, even though they may have to make concessions in the process.

You may think of negotiation in the context of industrial relations or of sales and purchasing. However, negotiation takes place in many other everyday work situations, and you will probably be negotiating if you are involved in getting your ideas or policies accepted or in brokering any kind of change.

Action checklist

1 Clarify your objectives

Before embarking on any kind of negotiation, however seemingly trivial, decide exactly what you are negotiating about and what the best outcome for you would be:

- Make sure that you are aware of all the issues at stake and their relative importance.

- Assess whether you can achieve your objectives without negotiation.

- Ask yourself whether there are any other, more effective ways of getting the same results.

- Work out which factors are negotiable – what are you aiming for, what can you give way on and how far? Define upper and lower parameters for an acceptable deal.

- Work out which factors are non-negotiable – these might be limits imposed by time, money, company policy, resources or legislation, forming a window within which you have to negotiate.

- Any deal that you hope to negotiate must be better than your BATNA (best alternative to a negotiated agreement). It is a good idea to work out a BATNA as a last resort. If negotiations fail and you still need to achieve your objectives, you may have to put this back-up plan into action.

2 Find out about the other parties in the negotiation

You may be negotiating with one person or several, from your own organisation or from others. Try to assess as precisely as you can what the other parties want from this deal, uncover any hidden agendas and anticipate how others may approach the negotiation. Remember to look for both hard information (facts and figures) and soft information (issues of strategy, personality, and so on).

Look for details of:

- the people with whom you will be dealing – factors to consider may include their working style, authority, internal company politics in which they may be involved, any personal interest they may have in the deal, and their level of commitment

- any other companies involved – try to assess their financial and market position, history, future plans, and the effects which your proposed deal may have on them

- any other parties, interest groups or representative bodies that the proposed deal might affect.

3 Examine your own position

Where do you stand in your company? What level of power and authority do you have? Do you have management and/or board support? You may find that you have to negotiate with your own side before you negotiate with outside parties to determine whether you start from a position of solidity or weakness.

Now you can:

● assess the advantages of a deal to the other parties and prepare to 'sell it sunny side up', emphasising the benefits to them rather than any disadvantages

● decide who needs to be present at the negotiation and who needs to be kept informed; if others are negotiating alongside you, brief your team and agree on the line you will be taking

● choose a negotiating style – a cooperative approach is usually preferable to confrontation. While you examine your own position, recognise that the other party (parties) has as many interests to defend and promote as you do. Try to work out what those interests are and consider the other party's BATNA. Acknowledge that there is probably no single answer and the best solution is one where there are gains for all the parties concerned.

4 Plan the exchange

Work out how you would like the exchange to progress. Make sure that the stages of the exchange are logical, and include contingency plans in case things fail to go exactly as planned.

If negotiations are taking place face-to-face and might be long or complex, prepare concise written notes that you can take in with you.

Discuss with other parties whether negotiations will be formal or informal. Consider opening with brief presentations from each side before launching into the bargaining process.

If the negotiation is complex, you may wish to prepare a detailed case statement (containing the facts and statistics of your case)

and share this with the other party or parties before the exchange begins. Make sure this is well presented.

Agreement will be easier when expectations are realistic. A negotiating team should not raise its own expectations while lowering those of the other team. The primary purpose is to find a 'door' rather than a 'wall'.

5 Plan the environment if a face-to-face meeting is involved

- Arrange a suitable date and time and allow adequate time. Bear in mind that follow-up meetings may be necessary.

- Make sure that the premises are suited to the purpose of the meeting.

- Pay attention to room layout, availability of technology (such as projectors), seating and refreshments.

6 Begin the exchange

After any introductions, outline the purpose of the meeting and the proposed agenda, copies of which should have been previously circulated to all parties.

7 Conduct the exchange

This part of the negotiating process involves both emotion and logic in a complex interaction. Your behaviour during the exchange will influence the success of your negotiation.

Conducting your case:

- State your case clearly and logically. Focus on your objectives and keep what you want from the deal uppermost in your mind. Avoid jargon or specialist vocabulary with which other people may be unfamiliar. If others use unfamiliar terms, do not be afraid to ask their meaning.

- Use questions when you need clarification or do not understand, and also as a means of progressing the negotiation. Effective negotiators have been shown to ask more than twice as many questions as ineffective negotiators.

- Look out for inconsistencies in the accuracy or logic of your opponent's arguments.

- Bear in mind your parameters and be honest and consistent about your bottom line. Constant lowering of this line will lead your opponent to keep pushing to see how low you will go.

- Be careful about what you put on the table, as once something has been offered there is no way of getting it back. Develop a form of words that allows an offer to be sounded out formally without giving it away for nothing. An example would be: 'If we were to offer xxx, would that be accepted?' If the answer is 'No', then the offer has not been made.

- If you make concessions, get something in return and try to avoid giving something for nothing.

  Conducting yourself:

- Try to keep stress to a minimum and keep yourself calm and composed.

- Speak or write with confidence and be assertive.

- Try to avoid behaviour that will annoy or offend (this can range from the trivial, such as clicking a pen repeatedly, to the serious, such as personal insults). It has been shown that the average negotiator does something that irritates the other party every six minutes.

8 Close the deal

This is often the most feared part of the negotiating process because it can make or break the deal. Intuition plays a part in a successful close, but you can improve the process in the following ways:

- Use conditions to try to find grounds for agreement and make trial, hypothetical proposals to sound out the other party; for example, 'Suppose I could guarantee a bulk order for the next few years, would it then be possible for you to lower the unit price?'

- Link different items together to create flexibility in the deal, but be sure that the resulting package is practicable.

- Keep additional concessions up your sleeve to bring out if they are needed to facilitate the close – but be careful not to compromise your bottom line.

- Make accurate summaries of the proposed deal so far, and make these more frequently as the close approaches. Clarifying the state of play will help to move the negotiation along.

- Do not take decisions when under extreme pressure or on the spur of the moment; if necessary, ask for an adjournment to consider your position.

- If the negotiation is going nowhere, you could suggest a recess or reconvention at a later date, impose a deadline, threaten to pull out, or appoint arbitrators.

9 Record the agreement

The deal must be in writing and signed by both parties. Even if the matter is seemingly unimportant, a record should be made of what was agreed:

- Keep accurate minutes. Get the other parties who were present to sign them as a record of what took place.

- Summarise the deal accurately. Specify all conditions (timing, personnel involved, resources required, etc) and define all terms used.

- Include an agreed implementation plan with a clear timetable, and consider including terms for cancellation.

- Ensure that everyone concerned is told about the agreement at the appropriate time. Think widely – depending on the importance of the issue, the people concerned could include your superiors, employees, colleagues, customers, trade unions, shareholders or the general public.

10 Implement the agreement

Make sure that the agreement is set in motion according to the schedule. Carry out the actions for which you are responsible promptly and efficiently, and make sure that others do likewise.

The implementation plan should also include review procedures to allow regular progress reporting and mechanisms to address any non-observance of the agreement.

11 Review your performance

How did you handle:

● the preparation?

● the exchange?

● the close?

● yourself?

What did you do right or wrong and how can you improve next time?

As a manager you should avoid:

● confusing consultation with negotiation – if you are not prepared to start bargaining, don't allow other parties to

● confusing coercion with negotiation – the process should not be one-sided, but mutually rewarding.

Robert B Cialdini
Influence and persuasion

Introduction

Robert Cialdini (b. 1945) is a social psychologist who has
undertaken extensive research on the psychology of influence,
persuasion and negotiation. He is the most cited living expert in
the field of persuasion research and is best known for his 1984
book on persuasion and marketing, *Influence: the Psychology of
Persuasion*. Over two million copies have been sold and it has
been translated into twenty-seven languages.

Life and career

Cialdini undertook his undergraduate education in psychology at
the University of Wisconsin and received his doctorate from the
University of North Carolina. Post-doctoral training at Columbia
University followed. He held visiting scholar appointments at Ohio
State University, the Universities of California at San Diego and
Santa Cruz, the Annenberg School for Communications, and at
the Psychology Department and the Graduate School of Business
of Stanford University.

Currently, Cialdini is Regents' Emeritus Professor of Psychology
and Marketing at Arizona State University, where he has also
been named Distinguished Graduate Research Professor. He has
been elected president of the Society of Personality and Social
Psychology, a US organisation, and is the recipient of many
awards, including the Distinguished Scientific Achievement Award

of the Society for Consumer Psychology, the Donald T Campbell Award for Distinguished Contributions to Social Psychology and the Peitho Award for Distinguished Contributions to the Science of Social Influence.

Cialdini has spent his career researching the science of influence. This has earned him an international reputation as an expert in the fields of persuasion, compliance and negotiation. Because of the global recognition of his research and his ethical business and policy applications, he is often regarded as the 'godfather of influence'.

The six universal principles of influence

Cialdini's six principles of influence were introduced in his book *Influence: the Psychology of Persuasion*. Although published some thirty years ago, the ideas within it are still valid and are used by businesses and organisations globally.

His interest in compliance led him to ask:

- What are the factors that cause one person to say yes to another person?
- Which techniques most effectively use these factors to bring about such compliance?

Cialdini's theoretical perspective is that to deal with a complex world, the human brain has evolved spontaneous or reflex responses to various phenomena.

The six principles play on primary human instincts and under normal circumstances are good traits, but they can be used against us by those who seek to exploit and influence us.

Cialdini hoped that by understanding these principles of persuasion, people would be better able to recognise situations in which they might be led to act against their will and would have the tools to resist unwanted social influence.

The six principles are:

- reciprocity
- commitment/consistency
- social proof
- authority
- liking
- scarcity.

Principle 1: reciprocation

The first principle states that humans are hardwired to want to return favours, pay back debts and treat others as they have been treated. In essence, we prefer to say yes. According to Cialdini, there is no human society that does not practise this rule of reciprocity. It is a cultural standard that obligates us to return favours, gifts and invitations.

The reciprocity principle recognises that we feel indebted to those who do something for us. This can lead us to feel obliged to offer concessions to others if they have been offered to us, in short to reciprocate, as we feel uncomfortable being indebted to others. If a colleague, for example, offers help to you when you are under pressure to meet a deadline, you may feel obliged to support them when they need help.

The reciprocity principle can be used for uninvited exchanges too. When this occurs the ability to freely decide is affected and people may be led to react automatically or involuntarily.

A defence against reciprocity would be to reject the initial offers or concessions. If you redefine them as tricks or ploys, you no longer feel obligated to respond reciprocally, unless you know the other person and can trust that the initial favour is given meaningfully.

Despite the strong influence that the principle may exert upon us, we have the ability to discern, adjust, or to say no in situations where we might be led to reciprocate.

Principle 2: commitment (and consistency)

Cialdini argues that humans have a desire to be consistent and that they also value consistency in others. Consistency is a powerful social influence which is highly valued by society. The principle of commitment declares that we have a need to be seen as consistent and to honour our commitments.

Once we have committed to something or someone, we are much more likely to go through and deliver on that commitment. So we would be far more likely to support a colleague's project proposal if we had expressed an interest when the idea was first raised.

To Cialdini, commitments have the most authority to influence someone when they are active, public, require effort and are internally motivated or uncoerced.

To counter this principle you should not allow yourself to be pressured into accepting requests that you do not want to perform, and you should disregard unjust or falsely obtained commitments. Cialdini asserts that you need to recognise the personal signals – including what he calls stomach signs and heart-of-heart signs – that can help you make the right choices.

Principle 3: social proof

This principle is related to safety in numbers or the wisdom of crowds. Primarily, Cialdini sees uncertainty as the cause of the behaviour behind this principle. When we do not know what to do we look to others for social cues to validate our own actions.

So, for example, if a colleague is working late, we may feel that we should also work late. Similarly, if we see that a restaurant is full of people, we may be more likely to eat in that restaurant.

This principle can be reinforced if we can relate to the people in question. So if your team members are active participants in team meetings, you may be encouraged to speak up too.

The principle of social proof leads us to believe that the greater the number of people who find an idea correct, the more the idea will seem to us to be correct.

To counter this principle it is important to recognise that the actions of others should not form the sole basis of your own actions.

Principle 4: authority

People generally have been taught to accept and to respect authority. We want to follow the lead of experts. Often, however, we commit to this tendency with little or no critical thinking on our part. It is all too easy for people to confuse the symbols of authority such as titles, appearance and possessions with true substance.

This acceptance of authority, though it allows a society or culture to operate smoothly, can also lead to authority abusing its power.

A defence against this principle would be to consider your reaction to authority figures and ask yourself if the person who has triggered your respect for authority genuinely has the authority they are displaying, or is merely using the symbols of that authority.

Principle 5: liking

Cialdini argues that we are more inclined to be influenced by people we like. If we like someone, we are more likely to do what they want or ask us to do. A salesman, for example, will try to befriend you and get you on his side before trying to sell you something.

Cialdini cited a number of factors which influence whether one person likes another. These included attractiveness, associations, compliments, similarities, flattery and common goals.

Persuasion experts take advantage of this principle by achieving positive associations with those they are trying to persuade, influence or manipulate. To put it bluntly, if someone wants something from you, they may compliment you.

The principle can be countered by separating the request from the requester and making decisions based on the merits of the offer, rather than on the emotional response that you may have about the requester. So even if you like the person, you must consider whether their offer is one that is really beneficial, rather than one that is based on your connection to them.

Principle 6: scarcity

The scarcity principle is extremely powerful and operates on the value or worth that people attach to things. In economic theory, scarcity relates to supply and demand. The less there is of something, the more valuable it can become as more people want it. Cialdini states that humans are challenged emotionally when freedoms are threatened and scarcity can limit free choice. This may cause people to want to try to possess the item more than ever.

People are generally susceptible to some form of this principle, as opportunities seem more valuable when they are less available and things that are difficult to achieve or out of reach are perceived as better.

To counter the effects of this principle you should try to step back and assess the merits of the opportunity or the value of the item in terms of why you would want it. Doing this will give an objective evaluation of its personal value, rather than overvaluing it because it is scarce or has the appearance of being scarce.

In perspective

When doing research for his book, Cialdini went under cover to observe real-life persuasion in action. He gathered information first hand and learned the tricks mastered by used-car dealerships, fund-raising organisations and telemarketing firms. His book has brought persuasion research to the forefront of psychology. Cialdini shares his findings with environmentalists, policymakers and business owners, inspiring them to use his principles of persuasion to reduce energy usage among industries and consumers.

In social settings it can often be difficult not to experience persuasion and influence. Advertising too is persuasive and plays on our freedoms and fears. The best defence against all the principles therefore is to be aware of them and to try to understand when they are being used.

Effective business writing

Business writing covers all forms of written communication in a workplace context, both electronic and paper-based. These include letters, memos, emails, public relations or marketing copy, contributions to social-media forums, brochures, web pages, newsletters, instruction manuals and reports.

Many different forms of written communication are used in the workplace, but the need to get the right message across to the right people at the right time is common to them all. If a communication is unnecessarily lengthy, confusing or difficult to understand, the chances are that readers will either fail to read it or, if they do read it, will fail to grasp the implications. This damages the ability of the organisation to operate effectively and could result in bad decisions, dissatisfied customers, lost sales or a failure to take advantage of new opportunities. This checklist focuses on documents such as reports or proposals, but it also provides an introduction to the basic principles that apply to all forms of business writing. It aims to help writers get the attention of their audience and communicate clearly and concisely.

Business writing should aim to inform, educate, interest, guide, motivate and influence the reader. This is achieved by explaining the aims and objectives of the communication, including facts, information and data, presenting findings and conclusions, making recommendations and proposing the next steps to take.

Action checklist

1 Be clear about your aims and objectives

Start by thinking about what you want to achieve; otherwise you will have no way of judging whether your communication has been successful. Make sure that you take the broader organisational context into account. Decide what you want to happen as a result of your communication. Do you want to impart facts or provoke a response? If you are expecting recipients to take action, make sure that you are explicit about what you expect or would like them to do. The communication should clearly state the aims and objectives from the outset in order to set the scene. Whatever form your writing takes, it should be appropriate to its purpose and its audience.

2 Check whether a written communication is really needed

Consider whether a written communication is the most appropriate format. Generally, you should only write if:

- you need to address a number of people
- the argument or explanation is complex or needs visual support
- you need a considered response
- you need an accurate and permanent record of the communication
- distance or availability makes a telephone call impractical.

If the message is urgent, one-to-one, or can be expressed simply and without visual aids, consider using the telephone. Alternatively, if you need to involve several people in an urgent decision, or if action is conditional on presenting an argument to several people, it may be necessary to organise a meeting. This could be a meeting in person, or via a telephone conference call or a video link.

3 Consider who should sign off the communication

The assumption is that you are writing the communication yourself. However, its effectiveness may depend on it being seen to come from someone else. The message may carry greater weight if it is approved or signed by someone more senior, or in some cases more junior. The important point is that the signature is of someone with the right credentials to address the target audience.

4 Determine the right audience

Consider whether the target audience is the right one. Are those to whom the communication is addressed in a position to deliver the action you need and will they have the motivation to respond? Do they represent the right constituencies within the organisation? Will they have the authority to act? If your communication is aimed at the public, how will you ensure that the right people see the report?

5 Set the right tone

Tone is crucial in gaining the attention and respect of your audience. Your choice of style will depend on two main factors: the audience you are addressing and the type of information you have to pass on. For example, are you making a progress report to the board or giving a briefing to your team? Are you presenting the benefits of a product or service to potential customers or providing technical information to a colleague? Think about what motivates your audience and what their expectations will be. Try to establish common ground and express the message in terms of the effect on you and on the recipients.

6 Build a convincing argument

If you are putting forward a proposal or attempting to influence your audience, develop a proposition that is compelling by spelling out the benefits and anticipating and forestalling objections. Look at the issue from the recipients' perspective, considering the concerns they may have, and show how the proposal addresses these and how it fits in with overall organisational strategy. Be realistic about problems and the effort required to overcome them. Prepare an outline of your communication by noting down the main strands of your argument in a few words, grouping key relationships and themes together in order to build a structure around them.

7 Structure your communication

Consider the most effective structure for the information you wish to communicate. Many forms of formal written communication, especially substantial reports, typically consist of:

- aims/objectives
- scope/parameters of the issue
- facts and information
- conclusions
- recommendations
- next steps.

The structure can be logical (a discussion of the issue, followed by evidence and conclusions) or declarative (the conclusion first, backed up by evidence). The structure may be determined by the recipient. For example, if you are hoping to pique the interest of senior managers, moving straight to the recommendations after first setting out the aims and objectives will get their attention even if they disagree with you. Feelings of curiosity, disagreement or consternation will make it more likely that they will engage with the rest of the document to ascertain whether the conclusions and recommendations are really supported by the facts presented.

If an executive summary is included, aim to keep it brief. As a rough guide, any document of eight pages or more should be accompanied by an executive summary of one page or less. Clarity and brevity are important aspects of any form of effective business writing, so this should be kept in mind at all times.

The sections of your document covering the conclusions, recommendations and next steps are critical, as your readers are likely to turn to these first. Effectively, they represent the end product. Conclusions, recommendations and next steps need to:

- meet the stated aims and objectives
- be drawn from the facts and information in the document
- be realistic and logical in relation to resource availability and organisational capabilities
- be brief and clear.

8 Guide the reader around your text

Use clear signposts and flags to catch your readers' eye and guide them regardless of the structure used or the level of formality. Provide an introduction that explains why you are writing and a summary that lists your key points, and separate out your conclusions and recommendations. This is particularly important for reports. Try to use section headings, as your audience may not have time to read the document in its entirety. Carefully worded headings should allow the audience to follow the argument simply by reading them alone.

9 Make your text easy to read and unambiguous

Think about readability. Use short paragraphs and short sentences and avoid words that may be unfamiliar to your audience. Use plain English. As a rule, avoid jargon. However, if you are writing for an internal or technical audience, some words and phrases that would be considered jargon to other audiences may be useful shorthand in what could otherwise become a wordy and lengthy document. Spell out abbreviations the first time you use them. Use tangible rather than abstract concepts and use the active rather than the passive voice ('he decided' rather than 'it was decided'), except where it is irrelevant or inappropriate to say who was responsible for the action. Use an occasional image to illustrate a point, but avoid language that is too flowery or informal. Humour is rarely appropriate in a formal document, but it can be persuasive in a team briefing. Taste in humour is subjective, so it is best to avoid it unless you know your audience well. Be grammatically correct and check your spelling.

10 Enliven your text with graphics

If appropriate, use graphics to back up your arguments and convey your messages – but only if they are clear and easy to understand. Tell your audience when to look at them (by notes in the text) and where to find them (with references to figure numbers). Include them in the body of the text, with the exception of detailed statistical tables, which should be placed in appendices at the end of the report. Do not be tempted to use statistical tricks to bolster a weak argument: for example, distorting the 'y' axis of a graph to paint a more favourable picture of a sales increase. The size of the graphic should be determined by what is needed for clarity and understanding. Consistency in how graphics are presented (size, positioning, use of colour, etc) throughout the document help make the document easy to follow.

11 Revise your text once it is complete

Your communication will be effective only if it is accurate and authoritative. Read through your draft and be critical, or ask someone such as a colleague who has not been involved in preparing the document to review the text. If this is not possible, put it aside for a while before reading it again yourself. Check that your reasoning and arguments follow a logical sequence; ensure that your facts are correct; cite the source and authority for any opinions given or make it clear that you are expressing your own opinion; give due weight to conflicting arguments; and cover alternative conclusions or recommendations without being too dismissive of them. Be as succinct as you can.

12 Check the presentation and layout of the text

As with oral communication, you are likely to be judged less on the content of your message than on its presentation. Are you using a clear, easy-to-read typeface and font size? If your communication is paper-based, are paper and print quality good? Use bold characters (sparingly) to give emphasis to key words and phrases rather than underlining, and make sure that there is enough white space around the page. Use indentation, bullet points and short one-liners to break up the text. If your organisation has a house style, be sure to apply it.

13 Follow up on your communication

If the communication is important, follow it up with a telephone call or face-to-face meeting to make certain that the reader received the message you wanted to convey. Ensure that there are no misunderstandings or ambiguities and that appropriate follow-up actions or responses are in progress.

As a manager you should avoid:

- errors of grammar and spelling
- lengthy sentences with multiple phrases and clauses
- inappropriate use of jargon or technical terms
- excessive use of rhetoric or humour.

Report writing

Reports are written documents or, in some cases, oral statements analysing a particular issue, incident, situation or proposal, usually including conclusions and recommendations for future action. This checklist focuses on the production of a written report.

Reports are a standard management tool and managers are frequently called upon to produce them. Although managers are expected to write reports, however, they are often not provided with any training in doing so. Writing a good report can make the difference between achieving and missing an objective. A clear, well-presented report can greatly assist in the process of planning and decision-making, but a report that is badly structured, uses inappropriate language or is poorly presented may confuse the reader and prejudice the outcome. So writing an effective report can make a significant contribution to business or organisational success. It can also be a means of impressing your superiors and improving your career prospects.

Anyone writing a report must keep the needs of the readership clearly in mind. A long-winded and lengthy document is unlikely to be welcome, especially if it is being presented to busy senior managers who need to gain an understanding of the subject but have limited time to devote to reading it. A sound structure with clear conclusions and/or recommendations and a short summary is crucial if a report is to achieve its objectives.

Report writing is not just a question of technical skill. Reports should be based on facts and evidence but are often intended to influence or persuade, so you need to consider how best to put your point of view across in a persuasive manner, particularly if the report is analysing a product or service that your organisation plans to develop or a new market that it is considering entering. Be aware, too, that you may be asked to write a report on something that is contentious or politically sensitive in your organisation. In such cases it is important to speak to all the relevant stakeholders at the evidence-gathering stage. Doing so will ensure that people feel that their views have at least been listened to, even if you come to a conclusion they disagree with. You must also make sure that you can justify any recommendations you make.

The same basic guidelines for report writing apply whichever type of report you are writing, whether it is a research report, staff appraisal report, accident report or a standard monthly report to management. This checklist looks at the key stages of successful report writing and is intended both for those new to report writing and for experienced report writers who wish to improve their style.

Action checklist

1 Define the purpose and objectives of the report

Putting pen to paper (or fingers to keyboard) is not the way to start the report-writing process. It is essential to plan what you are going to say if you want your report to be effective.

When preparing for the writing process you should consider:

- the terms of reference (definition of the task) or precise purpose of the report
- why the report is needed
- who will be reading the report
- the type of report required
- the scope of the subject to be covered

- the timescale in which it must be completed.

Make sure that you are clear about the intended readership, as this will help you pitch the report at the correct level. Will the person who requested the report be the primary reader? Who else will see it? How much do they know about the subject already? What do they need to know about the subject? What do they not need to know about the subject? What do they expect from the report?

The approach used to write a report will depend to some extent on the specific circumstances. A report outlining a particular proposal may not need to address counter-arguments, whereas other reports may need to present evidence and opinion on a range of different options.

Be sure to establish the objectives in your own terms so that you are clear about what is to be achieved. Taking a few minutes at the start of the process to think about the objectives may save you hours of work later.

2 Gather and organise the information

With most reports you will not have all the information you need to hand, so some form of research or data collection will be required. You will need to:

- decide what information you need
- collect the material
- collate and organise the information.

This may entail identifying and reading other reports, interviewing people, carrying out primary research or drawing data together from a number of different locations. Remember to consider both internal and external data sources and to consult the relevant people in your organisation, as this will not only add potentially useful information but also help them to feel involved.

Gathering too much information is not a serious weakness, but gathering too little definitely is. Bear in mind what you need the information for and how much time you have available to produce the report; otherwise you run the risk of information overload and may find yourself flooded with data that you may not need and do not have time to analyse properly.

3 Structure your report

Analyse the information you have gathered to identify what matters most and what provides supporting evidence. To achieve this you should refer back to your objectives and your readership.

Once you have decided on the content of your report, you need to determine the order in which to present what it says. To work out a logical order, it is helpful to organise your information into themes or to group individual pieces of information together under common headings. A well-planned structure can save you a lot of work, eliminate the need for explanatory notes referring to other parts of the report, and make things easier for writer and reader alike. Restructure the report if the order does not seem logical, or if it fails to convey the message you have in mind.

Plan the layout of your report following the house style of your organisation, if there is one. A simple framework can form the basis of most reports. This can be adapted for particular circumstances. Reports may consist of the following elements, although you may not need them all in every case:

- title or title page (including the date)
- executive summary (including a short statement of the conclusions and/or recommendations)
- contents list
- introduction (this sets the scene by providing background information and should include terms of reference and the methodology used, if appropriate)
- main body of the report
- conclusions
- recommendations

- references or bibliography
- supplementary evidence/appendices (including full tables and graphics that would clutter the main report).

A short report may not need to include a title page, but it must have a title. Contents listings are needed only for longer reports. A summary is useful in any report of more than a couple of pages. It should provide the reader with the main messages should they not have time to read the whole report.

4 Write the main body of the report

Once all the information has been collected, sorted, checked and organised, it must be translated into a readable report.

Put the report together initially as a draft, using your objectives to guide you. It may be helpful to write the report in a single sitting to keep your train of thought clear. The deadline will help you to focus.

Tips for writing the report:

- Write as you speak, but avoid slang, jargon and clichés.
- Avoid complicated language that your reader will not understand. When transferring the spoken word on to paper it is easy to make sentences too complicated. Adapt your style to suit the readership so that the report does not lose clarity or impact.
- Start a new paragraph each time there is a new line of thought. A mass of text with no or few paragraph breaks and limited white space on the pages is likely to be daunting for the reader.
- Avoid long and complex sentences – use short words and phrases for concision and clarity.
- Include only the information the reader needs to know.
- Use technical terms only where you have to or where you are sure that your audience will understand them. If necessary, include a glossary to assist your readers.
- Use bullet points or numbering where appropriate, to emphasise, or summarise information, but do not overuse them.

5 Draw conclusions and decide on recommendations

Senior managers and decision-makers reading a report on a specific proposal will expect it to give them a simple recommendation: should we or should we not go ahead? Generally, the person who writes the report will be deemed the best person to draw conclusions and make recommendations. Conclusions should not be seen as superfluous repetition but as a necessary reminder of the main points presented. Including them at the end means that the reader does not have to flick back and forth through the report to check what has been said earlier. It is usually best to present conclusions in a numbered or bulleted list.

Recommendations should also be included. If the conclusion is that nothing is wrong or that nothing needs to change, it is still important to state that no action is necessary at this stage. Recommendations may need to be no more than a simple statement, but multiple recommendations should be summarised. List recommendations in order of importance and make them realistic and achievable. Give timescales for completion.

It is at this point in the report that you are most likely to need to write persuasively. Make your recommendations and conclusions as specific as possible, use language which will get the reader's attention and emphasise the benefits of whatever approach you are suggesting. Be prepared to accept responsibility for the recommendations when signing the report. Remember that this is not just a technical exercise – some of your colleagues may find your recommendations hard to swallow, or even reject them outright, so be prepared to take a certain amount of flak. Stand up for your point of view and re-emphasise the evidence supporting the recommendations.

6 Include graphics

Graphics including line graphs, bar graphs, pie charts and pictographs, illustrations such as flow charts and photographs, and tables of data are invaluable for presenting complex information. They should be formatted with care, clearly numbered and titled, and referred to within the text. Consider which type of graphic will best express the information or message you wish to convey. If a graphic is included to help explain a particular point, it should be placed as close as possible to that point in the text. If it is supplied for documentary support, it can be placed in the appendices at the end of the report.

7 Review what you have written

Always allow time to review what you have written and make any necessary amendments. Most reports need to be completed by a specific date or within a stated time period, so aim to finish writing a day or so before the submission date. It is not ideal to review the report immediately after you have completed it. Revising it a day or two later can be more effective, as the ideas will still be clear in your mind, but the interval will give you perspective and help you read what you have written with a critical eye.

Take time to check that the report says what you want it to say and that the key points stand out clearly. Be sure to consider whether:

- it covers your objectives fully

- it is readable – if necessary make use of techniques such as Gunning's Fog Index or the Flesch Reading Ease Scale

- there is sufficient differentiation between conclusions drawn from factual evidence presented in the report and those based on your personal opinions

- recommendations for future action are based on the findings of the report.

In addition:

- check the overall structure of the report, particularly any cross-references

- check spelling, punctuation and grammar

- ask a colleague to proofread the report and to consider issues such as readability, structure, persuasiveness, clarity and objectivity.

8 Final checks and submission

First impressions are crucial. The presentation of the report will be the first thing the reader notices, and it needs to meet two main objectives:

- to make the report readable and accessible
- to make the structure and organisation of the report clear.

Readers will associate the qualities they see in the report with you. So if you wish them to see you as organised and professional, you need to make sure that these qualities are reflected in the report and its presentation.

House style may dictate how your report should be set out. If your organisation does not have a house style, consider the following points:

- font and size of type
- spacing and margins
- justification of lines and paragraphs
- page numbering
- presentation of titles and headings
- numbered sections
- starting each section on a new page (advisable for longer reports)
- use of colour if you include graphics (but consider potential printing costs)
- binding, if the report is printed (for example, staples, spiral or ring, treasury tags, etc).

Consider how your audience will read the report. Will they print it out or are they more likely to access it on a computer screen or a mobile device such as a tablet? This may influence how you choose to set out the report; for example, if people are using tablets, you will want to avoid excessive scrolling.

Aim to submit the report ahead of schedule and distribute it as appropriate. If you need to get it printed, check how many copies are required.

As a manager you should avoid:

- providing incomplete information
- writing with a lack of clarity
- allowing the report to become unnecessarily long
- omitting relevant but sensitive or inconvenient information
- including irrelevant information
- conveying a lack of confidence in the message you are trying to put across
- making the report too technical
- submitting the document late
- ignoring the organisational, political and personal consequences of the report and its recommendations.

Email etiquette

Email etiquette is the observance and communication of generally accepted standards of sense, grammar and politeness when sending email messages.

Email has become the mainstay of organisational communications over the past twenty years. More recently, it has been suggested that the development of communication and collaboration technologies such as instant messaging and virtual workspaces may lead to the decline or even death of email. Nonetheless, email is still a popular business communication tool and is widely used. It is, however, an easy tool to misuse. Ineffective use can lead to confusion, create a bad impression of the sender's organisation or even result in legal penalties. Poor email etiquette and practice can also contribute to more general stressors for managers, such as time pressures, poor communications, information overload and frequent interruptions.

As regular senders and receivers of email, most people at some point experience or send messages in haste that:

- are poorly written or nonsensical
- have missing words or incomplete sentences
- are either extremely abrupt or ramble endlessly
- are unclear in their meaning
- make the reader feel that the sender is being flippant, rude or even abusive.

Few individuals send emails like this intentionally, but

expectations of a speedy response encourage people to send messages that are too brief, too long, mistyped or poorly considered and give recipients a false or misleading impression of what is intended. The technology makes it all too easy to send an email without giving due attention to the text of the message, who will receive it and how it will be perceived. There have also been many well-documented instances of emails being forwarded unwisely.

This checklist aims to provide guidance for managers to help ensure that email messages sent by their teams make good sense, contribute to clear communications, give a good impression of individual employees and their organisation, and do not give rise to any unintended problems such as accusations of defamation or loss of business reputation.

Action checklist

1 Think about presentation and formality

It is advisable to take a considered approach to all business communications, including email messages. Email has often been seen as an informal mode of communication, but work-related messages represent the sender's organisation, so reasonably formal standards of presentation and language are recommended. You always should use some form of address and sign-off for any business messages and write in complete sentences. Most organisations have policies and guidelines on email use and presentation, so make sure that you know and abide by them. Bear in mind that although email may seem to be private and impermanent, companies often introduce policies advising employees that email communications sent from business addresses may be monitored. Messages are also often retained and traceable over set periods of time for valid business and legal reasons.

2 Consider how to open and close your message

To some extent, the form of address used will depend on the context, location and culture of both sender and recipient, and on how well those concerned know each other. If in doubt or when dealing with people from other cultural backgrounds, it is always advisable to use more formal options of address and sign-off.

In the UK, it is common practice to start a message with the recipient's first name if you already know them, or with the title and surname if the communication needs to be more formal. Some people can find this somewhat abrupt, especially if they are from different cultural backgrounds. The less formal 'Hi' or 'Hello' for those you know or who have contacted you initially may be more appropriate in some cases.

Sign off formally or less formally, in line with the form of address used at the beginning of the message. Traditionally, 'Yours faithfully' is used for formally addressed recipients whose names you do not know and 'Yours sincerely' for formally addressed recipients whose names you do know. However, more informal sign-offs such as 'Regards' or 'Best Regards' are becoming more widely used in email messages.

3 Include a signature line

Many companies have a standard email signature that should be used for all business messages. Signature lines should give the sender's name, job title, full company name, telephone number, email, web and postal addresses, and often also include corporate logos, strap lines and social-media links. In the UK it is a legal requirement under the Companies Act 2006 and the Companies (Trading Disclosures) Regulations 2008 for companies to provide the following details on all business correspondence including email messages: registered number, registered office address and where in the UK the company is registered.

4 Use good practice for written business communication

As with all effective written business correspondence:

- be brief and succinct, but warm and polite

- keep things simple and clear, focusing on one subject per message

- avoid using jargon, 'smileys', textspeak, unexplained acronyms or abbreviations

- always write in full sentences

- do not write whole words and sentences in capitals, as this is seen as electronic 'shouting'

- avoid using flashing text or other special formats

- use good grammar and punctuation, and check your spelling

- explain what your email is about – never assume recipients already know

- avoid demands for an urgent or immediate reply – just suggest that an early reply would be appreciated, if you need one

- be restrictive about copying in others (cc), and only copy in colleagues who are directly involved and need to be aware of the communication. If necessary, messages can always be forwarded to others at a later point.

Communicate only things that you would commit to paper, or would be happy for colleagues or outside contacts to see.

5 Structure your message in a logical way

Use a logical structure to present and support the sense of your message. The three-part format below is frequently advised:

- clarify your reason for sending an email

- give the facts

- conclude with appropriate, related actions, proposals or comment, as necessary.

6 Think carefully before sending and accessing emails

When meeting face-to-face with others, or speaking on the telephone, we naturally make use of various non-verbal cues, such as facial expression or tone of voice, to convey our full meaning and interpret that of others. Email messages, however, lack these non-verbal cues, so it is crucial to ensure that you express your thoughts clearly before sending your message, and that you interpret the messages of others carefully rather than jumping to hasty conclusions. Email messages can be quickly written and are easy to send unthinkingly, but once sent it is difficult to withdraw what has been said.

Reread and think about each message before sending it. Who will be reading the message and how may it be received? If you are feeling angry or upset, draft the message but don't send it. Reread it later, when you are feeling calmer and more rational. If you think the message reads negatively, consider rephrasing it or using a different means of communication to give your response.

It can also be tempting to read every email as soon as it arrives, regardless of how unimportant or low-priority it may be. Disciplining yourself to handling email only at set times of the day will help you to manage your time more effectively and concentrate on the task at hand, rather than being subject to continual interruptions and distractions.

7 Make good use of the subject line

Always use the subject line appropriately. Most people receive lots of emails, and prioritising them can be hard (especially after a period away from work). Save recipients' time by clearly wording subject lines to give a good sense of the nature, purpose and relevance of the message. However, keep subject lines short and to the point.

8 Avoid strings of messages, where possible

A 'history' of previous messages in a string of communications may be helpful in some contexts (for a long-running discussion, for example, or in some group communications). But for new subjects, or if a new communication does not relate back to previous messages, avoid sending a string of messages. When forwarding messages, it is easy to end up sending unnecessarily long ones that may become confusing. Remove extraneous information before forwarding a message, and include only that which is relevant to the immediate recipient.

9 Take care with group messages

When sending group messages, retain the thread by ensuring that you keep the same subject for all replies to the group, or to individuals within it. Do not, however, reveal the email addresses of all group members in the address field, unless they know each other well enough to accept this (for internal use) or have given explicit consent for their email addresses to be revealed (for external recipients). This is important as email addresses can be used both deliberately and inadvertently by marketing agencies or by automated spam mailers. In the UK, it is a breach of data-protection legislation to pass on email addresses to people without permission. Avoid this by addressing the message to yourself and putting all the recipients in the bcc (blind carbon copy) field to protect their privacy. Never reuse someone else's cc (carbon copy) field to send a message, especially one that comments adversely on another person – they or their friends may be included in the list.

10 Use 'urgent' markers sparingly

'Urgency' flagging is useful to draw attention to messages that need to be read quickly, or require an urgent response, but it should not be used too readily. If a message really is important, consider using the telephone or meeting the recipient face-to-face, as emails are not always dealt with at once and people do not always use 'out of office' messages when they are away from their desks. Similarly, avoid the routine and unnecessary use of both 'delivery receipt' and 'read receipt' facilities.

11 Avoid humour, irony or sarcasm

Some people may know you well enough not to misread or misunderstand your messages, but in a business context, humour and irony are best avoided, and sarcasm should not be used at all. The use of humour or sarcasm is also highly culture-specific and may be understood very differently in different cultural contexts.

12 Check before sending large attachments

Large attachments can cause problems, as some organisations and email service providers limit the size of files that can be sent or received. Check with recipients before sending large files, or, if feasible, send a link though which the file can be accessed rather than attaching the document itself.

Refrain from forwarding chain letters, messages about hoaxes, or messages with attachments that you have not safely opened. Inform others at once if you discover that your computer is infected by a virus, as some malware programmes can access your address book and send messages to all the addresses listed.

13 Ensure clarity of ownership and legality

It is important to avoid confusion about the authorship of and authority for messages. You should never send emails in someone else's name, use another person's email account, or allow others to use your email account.

Be aware of the requirements of copyright law and do not reproduce copyright material in your messages without permission and acknowledgement. If your message includes text composed by another person, make this clear, and explain any changes or amendments you have made.

In addition to copyright, email messages are subject to all the other laws covering written communications. These include legislation on:

- wrongful discrimination
- obscenity
- data protection
- freedom of information
- defamation of character
- fraudulent misrepresentation
- display of registered company name and other details (as mentioned in point 3 above).

  Messages should be treated as 'instant letters' that may become public. Email etiquette and legal responsibility go hand-in-hand. It is easy to cross a line without intending too, possibly just by using 'reply all' and 'send'. So do be mindful of any risks before sending your messages.

14 Keep your inbox in order

Respond promptly to messages, and delete or file all messages received after reading them. Create subject folders to hold messages you need to retain, with a separate file for attachments sent and/or received. When sending and receiving emails with attachments, it is good practice to file these separately from the email itself (or delete them once read) to relieve the burden on your email program and save storage space in your inbox.

As a manager you should avoid:

- replying too quickly to messages that anger or upset you
- sending irrelevant or over-expansive messages
- making personal comments about others in email messages
- underlining in emails (this normally indicates a hypertext link in the online environment)
- using capital letters, as these are regarded as shouting
- copying people on messages unnecessarily

- using email for sending classified or otherwise sensitive material
- using email instead of personal contact for personnel management issues
- ignoring the inherent legal implications of poor email use.

Dale Carnegie
How to win friends and influence people

Introduction

Dale Carnegie (1888–1955) is best known for his work on the basic yet essential principles for dealing with people successfully. His common-sense advice included never criticising, complaining about or condemning another person, giving sincere appreciation to others, and stimulating in others a specific desire in order to motivate them.

Such advice formed the basis of the best-selling book for which Carnegie has become famous, *How to Win Friends and Influence People* (1936). In it Carnegie gives simple rules on how to achieve success with people, with examples of his own and others' experiences and historical stories about people such as Roosevelt and Lincoln. Although he is mainly known for this particular book, Carnegie began his career training people to become speakers and writing various other books. He produced some of the earliest self-improvement manuals, and these are still popular today.

Carnegie's main focus is on interpersonal skills, effective communication and being a successful salesperson.

Life and career

Dale Carnagey (he later changed his name to Carnegie) came from a poor farming family in Missouri and struggled through teaching college. Looking for a way to distinguish himself, he began to enter speaking contests and, despite a shaky start, was soon winning most of the contests he entered. Upon leaving college, he worked as a salesman and tried writing novels. He also became an actor temporarily, but eventually he decided to teach public speaking.

Carnegie's first courses on public speaking were run purely on commission, as he was initially refused any pay. The courses did well, however, and their popularity made him a great success. His first collection of writings, published in 1926, was *Public Speaking: a Practical Course for Business Men*. In 1936, Simon & Schuster published *How to Win Friends and Influence People*, which became a bestseller, selling over five million copies just in Carnegie's lifetime. He went on to write many popular books and founded the Carnegie Institute of Effective Speaking and Human Relations.

Key ideas

Carnegie believed that criticism should never be used, because people who are criticised tend to respond by justifying themselves and condemning the critical person in return. Great leaders such as Abraham Lincoln, Carnegie believed, achieved their success partly because they never criticised others. Instead, Carnegie recommended the practice of self-control, understanding and forgiveness. Most importantly, he advised that we should always try to see the other person's point of view. In order to influence people and achieve our aims, Carnegie suggests, it is necessary to understand individual motivation. Work on the art of persuasion, and ask yourself what will motivate a person to want to do a task for you. Carnegie considered that most people are interested only in their own desires, and when given what they want they can help the giver to achieve great success in business.

Using anecdotal evidence, Carnegie illustrates how nourishing a person's self-esteem can achieve far better results than criticism. For most people, he considers, the desire to be important is a main motivator, and can inspire them to do great things, such as become important leaders or make their fortune in business. On a smaller scale, people may want to drive a better car or buy a bigger house. Sometimes individuals may even become invalids to gain attention, or become insane so that they can live in their own dream world, where their importance can be exaggerated by imagination.

The rules

In *How to Win Friends and Influence People*, there are 'In a nutshell' conclusions at the end of each part of the book, where Carnegie summarises the main messages in terms of behaviour. Some of these are paraphrased below.

Six ways to make people like you:

1 Show a genuine interest in other people

2 Be happy and positive

3 Remember that people love hearing the sound of their own name

4 Listen to other people and develop good listening skills

5 Talk about others' interests rather than your own

6 Give others a sincere sense of their importance

Twelve ways to win people to your way of thinking:

1 To get the best of a situation, avoid arguments

2 Always listen to others' opinions and never tell anyone they are wrong

3 Admit it if you are wrong

4 Show friendliness

5 Make statements that the other person agrees with

6 Let the other person talk more than you

7 Make the other person feel that an idea is their own

8 See the other person's point of view

9 Show empathy with others' ideas and desires

10 Infuse some drama into your ideas

11 Appeal to the better nature of others

12 Finish with a challenge

Nine ways to change people without arousing resentment:

1 Start with genuine praise and appreciation

2 Draw attention to their mistakes gradually

3 Admit that you have made mistakes and then talk about theirs

4 Don't give direct orders but ask questions

5 Never humiliate anyone, and let people keep their pride intact

6 Use plenty of genuine praise and encouragement on the slightest improvement

7 Give people a reputation to maintain

8 Encourage them. Show them that their task is easy to correct

9 Suggest what you want them to do and make them happy about it

How to become a good public speaker

Carnegie is well known for his self-help guides. He taught his students how to interview well, make persuasive presentations and forge positive relationships. He also taught social and communication skills. Most successful were his self-help guides and lessons on how to be a public speaker, including advice on how to prepare, how to have confidence and how to deliver a speech effectively. Some of this advice is summarised below.

Speech preparation, Carnegie suggested, should generate an enthusiasm within yourself for public speaking, whether you have a financial or a social goal in view. Begin planning as soon as you can, and look for a topic that you know a lot about. Think about your talk at every possible opportunity, and research it thoroughly, using libraries and other sources and collecting more material than you will need.

Do not memorise your talk word-for-word, he advised, as you will be more likely to forget it, and it will also lose much of its effectiveness. Have plenty of material prepared, but try not to say too much during the talk itself.

Carnegie recognised that most people are nervous about talking in public. He suggested that if you try to act bravely and pretend that you feel more confident than you really do, you will often gain confidence. Practice will help you feel more certain of yourself, and it is a good idea to rehearse your speech as much as possible.

Speech delivery

Carnegie advised dressing the part for your talk, making sure you smile and are clearly visible to your audience. Show respect and affection for the audience, and let the first sentence capture their attention.

Use statistics or the testimony of experts to support your main ideas, but know your audience. Be eager to share your talk with your listeners, putting passion into your words and using your emotions without fear. Represent things visually when possible, turning a fact into a picture to help your audience understand what you are talking about and using specific instances and concrete cases.

Stress important words, and avoid hackneyed expressions or clichés. Once your talk is launched, you may feel freer to be humorous when appropriate.

Your talk should have some marked form of closure. Summarise what you have said, then use a finalising climax or close of some sort that is appropriate within the context, for example:

- appeal for action

- pay the audience a sincere compliment
- raise a final laugh
- give a fitting verse of poetry or a quotation.

Carnegie's concluding advice:

- Remember that many famous speakers were originally terrified of speaking in public and that a certain amount of stage-fright is useful.
- Predetermine your mind to success and seize every chance to practise.
- By increasing your experience your fear will lessen, so seek opportunities to speak in public, and believe in yourself.

In perspective

Carnegie claimed that his methods do really work and that he had seen them transform the lives of many people. Some management writers, however, such as Stuart Crainer, have dismissed his ideas as being simple wisdom dressed up in a commercial coating.

Certainly Carnegie's ideas are based on common sense and are hardly revolutionary. All his self-help books are based on down-to-earth and simply illustrated basic principles. Despite this simplicity, Carnegie has expressed many general truths that people acknowledge, and, whatever his critics may say, the books he wrote were influential, and they are still popular and regularly updated. His seminal work, *How to Win Friends and Influence People*, has sold more than twenty million copies throughout the world. An update in 2011, *How to Win Friends and Influence People in the Digital Age*, considered Carnegie's thinking in the light of social media and email. Carnegie created a highly successful business out of his ideas and today the global training organisation which still bears his name delivers training in over eighty countries.

It is possible to see Carnegie's influence in more recent ideas about management, particularly in discussions on the treatment of customers, and in approaches to interpersonal skills development. His focus on topics such as understanding motivation, effective communication, and the importance of relating to others and of gaining people's trust is just as relevant today.

Designing questionnaires

A questionnaire is a structured list of questions designed to gather information from a specific group of survey or research respondents for a specific purpose.

Questionnaires may be administered in various ways, including face-to-face interview, telephone, post, email or the internet. They may be structured (using closed questions with pre-coded answers), unstructured (using more open questions, so that respondents can phrase their own answers), or a combination of the two.

The questionnaire is a crucial part of most surveys, and its design and approach should relate to the main research question addressed by the survey and the research method being used.

Questionnaires are a useful tool for obtaining information to assist managers in the running of an organisation and in making business decisions. For example, questionnaires can be used to gauge the opinions and attitudes of employees, measure the satisfaction of customers or clients, or carry out market research.

However, care must be taken in the design and administration of questionnaires if the results are to be reliable and accurate. The design of a questionnaire should not be undertaken lightly, and expert advice may be desirable, if not essential, to avoid obtaining biased results or misinterpreting the findings. This checklist outlines the main points to take into consideration when putting together a survey to assess the opinions or attitudes of a particular group. It will also be helpful in providing background knowledge of the processes involved to those who use an external agency to carry out such a survey.

There are a growing number of web-based tools which can be used to help with the design of questionnaires. This checklist does not attempt to evaluate such tools, but it may provide an understanding of some of the fundamental issues for those considering using survey software programs.

Action checklist

1 Relate the questionnaire to the research objectives

The research study objectives provide the framework that determines the contents of the questionnaire. Consider the precise information you need and which variables should be covered. Questions to consider include: Which topics are relevant to the objectives? What information is imperative and what is just 'nice to know'?

For example, questionnaires can be used to measure:

- consumption patterns/market trends/reasons for market changes
- beliefs about specific products or services
- expectations related to specific products or services
- attitudes – general and specific
- motivations for behaviour – economic/psychological/social
- influences
- competitors' activities
- media exposure and influence.

Most questionnaires also classify respondents by factors such as age, sex, income, occupation or geographical area, so that the responses can be broken down and analysed in a variety of ways.

2 Consider the sample population you wish to select

Think about sources of names and contact details, such as internal or external databases, directories or commercial lists. Consider the balance of the sample: customers to non-customers, gender, socio-economic groupings and age if relevant. Samples may be selected by quota or randomly from the population to be surveyed. In theory, random samples are best, because it is possible to calculate any error in the sample. Pressures of cost, convenience and time, however, favour quota sampling, where interviewers are set targets to achieve, based on strata within the population.

When considering the sample, you should bear in mind any legal or ethical issues that may be involved.

3 Select the most appropriate distribution method

As mentioned above, questionnaires can be administered in various ways: post, telephone, fax, email, on the internet or face-to-face. Each of these has advantages and disadvantages and the most appropriate will depend on, for example, the subject of the survey, the nature of the survey population and the research budget available.

The following questions should be considered:

- Which delivery method is most likely to reach and/or be acceptable to the target group?
- Which method will enable you to recruit the most representative sample?
- Which is likely to give you the best response rate?
- How much time will be required to distribute the questionnaire and gather the responses?
- How complex are the questions you wish to ask?
- Do you need the level of personal interaction provided by a face-to-face interview or is it more important to avoid interviewer bias?
- What costs will be incurred?

- What resources will be needed in terms of time and personnel?

  Email can be suitable for short interviews, limited budgets, employee research, recruiting for internet-based questionnaires and business-to-business research. The internet may be more suitable for longer surveys, complex routing, consumer research and website tests.

  Email and internet surveys incur no postage or interviewer costs, can be faster than using the telephone, and can reach international audiences at no extra charge. Data collection is automated and these types of surveys do not suffer from interviewer influence. There are, however, some drawbacks, such as technical incompatibilities, the lack of a universal email directory, time delays in completion and return, self-selecting samples and low penetration of the population. With internet surveys there may also be less control over the sample population, with a reliance on the survey being 'found' on the website leading to sample bias.

4 Work out what you are going to do with the results

It is important to think about this from the outset. Anticipate the range of responses you are likely to receive and how these will be represented in the analysis. Even a low response may result in lots of paper to sort, or lots of data to key into an analysis package, spreadsheet or database. Irrespective of whether the analysis is to be done manually or electronically, think in advance about the ease or difficulty of data management and the facilities available to analyse responses. It may be worthwhile drafting a template for the analysis before drafting the questions themselves. However, do not focus on ease of analysis to the extent that it affects ease of use for the respondent, or the relevance of the results to your purpose. Working out how you will use the responses also helps to determine the mix or levels of structured and unstructured questions, and whether all questions will apply to all respondents. Will you need a filter question(s) to establish whether respondents are users or non-users of the product or service being surveyed, for example?

5 Determine the sequence of questions

It is good practice to:

- start with one or two general questions which are easy to answer
- explore present behaviour (for example, what is being used/done/ bought now) before asking about the past or future
- follow a logical order so that respondents are not confused
- position sensitive questions towards the middle or the end
- ensure that ideas which may influence answers to questions are not put into the respondent's head
- leave 'classification' questions to the end (for example, 'Which age range do you fall into?').

6 Design precise questions

Once you have determined the topics to be covered and the level of detail needed, you can draft specific questions. The following points should be taken into consideration.

Open or closed?

Questions can be closed (as in structured questionnaires) or open-ended (unstructured questionnaires). The anticipated answers to a closed question are pre-coded with simple instructions to the interviewer or respondent, i.e. 'Circle number' or 'Please tick ONE box only' or 'Please tick as applicable'. Allow for 'Don't know' or 'Not stated'. It is advisable to pre-code as many questions as possible: open-ended questions may provide richer data in that respondents answer in their own words, but the answers will still need to be put into coding categories afterwards.

Confusion and understanding

Avoid long, technical words and jargon with which your respondents may be unfamiliar. Watch out for any possible ambiguities or lack of clarity. Words such as 'frequently', 'often', 'regularly' or 'usually' need to be qualified. Avoid double negatives: 'Would you not drink a non-alcoholic beer?' Ask one question at a time – avoid questions such as 'What do you think of the economic policies of this government and how do you think they should be modified, if at all?' It is also important to avoid leading questions that direct the respondent towards a preferred answer.

Attitude questions

The simplest approach is to write statements and ask respondents to indicate whether they agree or disagree. For example:

'There is a sensible balance between my work and my personal life'

Agree 1 Disagree 2 Neither agree nor disagree 3 Don't know 4

This lacks sensitivity, however, as it gives no idea of how strongly those who reply 'agree' do agree, or how strongly people disagree. To measure the strength or weakness with which an attitude is held, rating scales should be constructed. Two commonly used types are Likert and semantic differential.

Likert. A statement is put to respondents, who are asked to indicate how much they agree or disagree with it.

For example: 'I have good opportunities for career development.'

Strongly agree 1   Slightly agree 2
Neither agree nor disagree 3   Slightly disagree 4
Strongly disagree 5

The responses are analysed by allocating weights to scale positions. You might allocate 5 points for 'strongly agree', 3 points for the mid-point and 1 point for strongly disagree or vice versa, but you must be consistent. If the scale range includes both positive and negative attitude statements, then 'strongly agree' for a negative statement rates 1, not 5.

Semantic differential. This scale is easier to administer and more meaningful when rating responses about the specific attributes of named products and services. For example, if the product is a motor car, you might construct the following double-ended scales:

Acceleration: Good .... Poor

It is also common to use points, for example:

Reliability: Good 1 2 3 4 5 Poor

Semantic scales can be either mono-polar (bitter – not bitter; modern – not modern) or bi-polar (modern – old-fashioned; strong – weak).

Length of questionnaire

The longer the questionnaire, the more likely it is that respondents will become fatigued and fail to complete it. It has been said that questionnaires should be as long as necessary and as short as possible. Avoid collecting any information that is not needed.

7 Consider design and page layout

Avoid a cramped layout and leave ample room for the answers. Leaving good borders and white space between the questions on the page or screen layout will ensure that the questionnaire is clear and easy to follow. Check, too, that the instructions are clear and that there is no room for confusion. Presenting the instructions in a different typeface (such as bold, underlined, upper case or in brackets) will help them stand out from the questions themselves. If the questionnaire is to be administered by an interviewer, clear instructions must be provided. An attractive layout is particularly important in a postal questionnaire, as it has been shown to have a significant effect on the response rate.

Remember to stress that answers given are in confidence and will be treated confidentially.

8 Pilot the questionnaire

It is important to pilot the questionnaire. Things that seem obvious to you may not be as clear to those completing the questionnaire. A pilot study will expose any ambiguities in the questions or the instructions and help you to clarify and refine them. It could also identify problems with layout, formatting or the order of the questions. A group discussion or a number of in-depth interviews could precede the larger fieldwork programme. A questionnaire could be tested by as few as ten interviews, although the more the better.

As a manager you should avoid:

- forgetting the 'nuisance factor' for the recipient
- saying it will take five minutes if it is likely to take fifteen minutes
- forgetting to thank respondents for their cooperation
- making the questionnaire too long and complicated.

Writing a business plan

A business plan is a written document that describes the business, sets out its aims and objectives, and makes a statement of intent for the future development of the business.

It may be helpful to think of a business plan as a roadmap to guide you through the process of developing a business. You need to keep in mind:

- the origin of the journey and its destination – you will have a guide to reach the final destination, but you need to be prepared to make adjustments on the way in response to the realities of the journey
- a justification of why the journey should be made – and the benefits of doing so
- the route options available for the journey, based on factors including journey time and conditions.

A business plan is exactly what the phrase suggests – a plan for the business – and every business should have one. A business plan can be used as a communication tool to highlight strategy and direction within a business, set targets for managers, and elicit the confidence and support of employees, shareholders and customers.

The process of drawing up a business plan provides an opportunity for business leaders to appraise the current situation, reach a common understanding of the challenges they face, set direction and identify options for the future – and then share that understanding with staff and stakeholders. The business plan provides a roadmap for action and a benchmark against which to measure progress. In larger organisations it can form the basis for divisional or departmental plans and be integrated with the process of performance assessment. A business plan can also give employees and stakeholders the opportunity to engage with the future direction of the organisation and identify additional areas for organisational growth.

Large corporations may produce an overall strategic business plan, but small businesses can benefit from producing a more specific business plan to assist them operationally. However, a business plan should not be targeted solely at those within the business who will implement it – it is also an important communication document for those outside the business, including shareholders and potential investors. It is particularly important for a business start-up to have a solid, well-researched business plan, which includes all the elements of a standard business plan but also has sections on market entry strategy and costs, and information on existing competitive products/services in place of historic performance figures. If an entrepreneur or business owner is seeking finance from investors or bankers, the business plan will demonstrate that the organisation has a realistic view of its current position and future development.

There is no single format for producing a business plan, and the structure may vary depending on the type and size of business and the context. All managers should bear in mind that their companies or external partners may well have their own guidelines or templates for business plans. These should be checked in conjunction with this checklist, which is aimed primarily at a start-up or a smaller business looking for funding. It outlines the main areas that should be covered in the plan and the steps taken to produce it.

Drafting a business plan requires:

- assessing the present internal and external position of the business and its prospects for the future

- analysing the market in which the business operates or plans to operate
- producing projections for up to five years, depending on the industry
- setting short-term and long-term objectives
- establishing a framework and processes for achieving objectives
- detailed research, careful thought and application
- clarity of expression to avoid misunderstandings, or possible conflict or confusion
- an honest and realistic appraisal of the business that includes organisational shortcomings, problems and obstacles, as well as positive factors.

The plan should be written from the reader's point of view, not the writer's, and needs to be accepted by, not just imposed on, the principal players in the organisation. It should be monitored and modified regularly, as appropriate, rather than just sitting on a shelf – it is a live document that drives the business forward.

A business plan should cover the following elements:

- **Operations** – including the supply of raw materials, technological requirements, key processes, resource needs, and production and delivery targets, as well as business processes, intellectual property, location and risk management.
- **Marketing** – how market intelligence will be gathered to ensure that the organisation's strategies will meet market needs and marketing objectives.
- **Finance** – an assessment of fixed and variable costs and minimum financial requirements. This should also include a detailed cash flow and profit forecast.
- **Human resources** – including recruitment, retention, compensation, leadership of the business and stakeholder relationship management.

Action checklist

1 Before you start

Gathering the relevant information is a good way to start thinking about why the business plan is being produced and what it needs to cover. It is often valuable to carry out a SWOT (strengths, weaknesses, opportunities, threats) analysis of your organisation and/or the sector concerned before beginning to draw up your plan. This will provide a picture of the current situation, help to generate strategic options and guide the formulation of objectives. Bear in mind that the analysis need not be restricted to the past and present; it can include the future, especially in terms of markets, customers and technology.

Also consider carrying out an assessment of the business environment using a PEST analysis or one of its variants to gain a broad perspective of potential influences and factors that will affect the organisation. PEST analysis covers political, economic, social and technological factors; PESTLE and LoNGPEST (local, national and global) also consider legal and environmental factors. This analysis will highlight opportunities and threats that need to be included in the results of the SWOT analysis.

You also need to carry out a market analysis covering:

- the overall market and the specific market segment(s) targeted
- detailed information on current and potential customers
- names of leading competitors, market share, alternative products or services
- routes to market
- market influences – economic and cultural trends, seasonal fluctuations, legislation, social factors, pricing movements and history
- information about suppliers of goods you wish to market – quality, resources, availability and competitive advantage
- market – you may find the five forces model developed by management guru Michael Porter will help you to carry out

a market analysis. The five forces are: existing competitors; potential new market entrants; similar competing products; customers; and suppliers.

The market analysis will enable you to identify market opportunities for your products and services as well as potential difficulties.

2 Provide background information

Describe:

- the current vision/mission/purpose of the business and the core values that form the foundation of its culture
- the ownership of the organisation, i.e. legal structure (limited company, partnership etc); include details of how much investment has already been made and by whom
- what differentiates the business from its competitors
- the history of the business and its products or services
- who the customers are and the market served
- past and current business performance
- factors that might affect the success or failure of the products or services
- the skills and experience of the organisation's key individuals or management team.

3 Define the objectives

Include a list of specific short-term targets that will help to indicate progress towards longer-term ones. Identify objectives for each of the business elements (operations, marketing, finance and HR). Measurability is important, so key performance indicators should be identified. Consider the use of tools such as SMART (specific, measurable, attainable, relevant and time-oriented) objectives and the balanced scorecard when defining objectives. Performance measurement should be integrated with individual performance appraisal. Always consider including a contingency plan outlining what to do if the objectives are not achieved.

4 Describe market opportunities

You need to convince readers or investors that the products or services will secure a substantial market, so this section should demonstrate that you are aware of what your target market is and what changes are affecting it. This is the place to outline the results of your market analysis and explain the opportunities and routes to market that have been identified.

5 Describe your plans for development and production (the operations plan)

Focus on all aspects of researching, developing, producing and delivering your products or services. Describe the research, development and production processes and the expected costs of raw materials, labour, plant and equipment, if relevant. Include a brief section on contingency planning in case things do not go according to plan. In this section you can also review location and risk-management issues as well as IT systems, including any hardware and software required. Are you aware of the terms and conditions of your main suppliers? Are you clear about the steps you need to take to maintain quality? As appropriate, explain how what you have learned from previous experience has informed/ shaped/pinpointed the steps that you intend to take in the future.

6 Propose your marketing strategy approach (the marketing plan)

Describe the marketing strategy you will use to take your products or services to market. Cover all the elements of the marketing mix, including the 7Ps of marketing:

- Price – pricing strategies and packages
- Place – distribution channels
- Product – unique features and benefits that differentiate your products and services
- Promotion – positioning, brand image and values, advertising and publicity materials

- People – the skills required to meet customer needs
- Process – the processes needed to deliver products and services and satisfy customers
- Physical evidence – the environment in which your products will be presented.

7 Clarify the current financial situation (the financial plan)

Clarify exactly what the plan requires of budget holders and/or potential investors. The financial plan is composed principally of figures for past, present and projected performance, including any start-up costs, profit/loss statements, cash-flow analyses and balance-sheet data. Repayment, or return on investment, will be of particular interest to investors, so include accurate break-even projections. Use financial ratios to analyse profitability, solvency and debt status. Include a comparative analysis of major competitors together with a rationale for any significant underperformance compared with competitors.

It is also important to demonstrate how sound financial control will be exercised over borrowed and incoming funds. Use financial ratios and break-even analysis to gain a clear understanding of the financials. Lenders like to see projected turnover and profit on each main product line or service, and they expect managers to concentrate on increasing sales of the most profitable lines identified. Make sure that you can support your sales forecast with reasons for your assumptions and opt for caution rather than the rosiest scenario. Can the business realistically support the level of borrowing or investment needed to realise the proposal?

8 Explain human resources issues (the HR plan)

Describe the strengths, skills and experience of all those involved, including the leadership characteristics of the executive team. If you include an organisation chart, it should show capabilities as well as responsibilities. If there are weaknesses, explain how these will be dealt with. The compensation structure of the organisation should be discussed here, along with recruitment and retention, and possibly also training and development strategies. Include details of how individual/group performance measurement is linked to strategy.

9 Cover risks, problems and critical success factors

Do not omit negative factors, either actual or potential. Demonstrate that you are aware of changes that are likely to affect areas such as markets, economic circumstances and information technology. Show that you are ready to correct any overspending or failure to meet deadlines, and demonstrate your recognition of the flexibility or contingency required. Provide a brief account of critical success factors such as:

- a learning environment that generates success
- specialists and technicians with their knowledge and networks
- the team's ability to respond to adversity and turn things round.

Include a sensitivity analysis showing the impact of variances in the main assumptions on financial performance.

10 Conclude with the key message

Consider the final impression you want the reader to have and make sure that this comes across in the conclusion. Summarise the key points: strategic direction, strengths, unique features and benefits, and (realistic) projections of sales and returns. Check that the summary is in line with the rest of the report and include a proposed timetable of events to demonstrate sound planning. Finally, check for correct grammar and spelling and the clarity of the language used.

11 Consider what you should include in appendices

The plan should be as concise as possible if it is to be effective. In general, the plan should not be more than 25–30 pages long, depending on its purpose, scope and scale, and the strongest focus should be on the management, marketing and financial elements. Place additional detail in appendices at the end of the plan. These should provide explanatory information, additional background information and evidence to support claims made in the body of the plan. They may include tables of data, financial reports and forecasts, independent reviews, research findings, CVs of key personnel and, where appropriate, technical specifications, details of any patents owned and a glossary of terms.

12 Provide an executive summary

The executive summary is perhaps the most important element of the plan, as it appears at the front of the document and will be read before anything else. Indeed, the summary may be the only part that is read, so it needs to engage the interest of the reader and encapsulate the contents of the plan clearly. For this reason, it should be written last. The reader should feel convinced that you fully understand your business proposition and have clearly identified how to manage requirements, risks and rewards going forward.

Include in the executive summary:

- the principal sensitivities and risks and the unique features of the product(s) or service(s)
- the current, mid- and long-term direction of the organisation
- the product/service benefits to the defined market sector
- the qualities and skills of the people who will make it all happen
- a financial statement of assets, the objectives, sales/profits expectations and how much capital is required
- a statement of the return for an investor, including comparison with main competitors.

As a manager you should avoid:

- skimping on research
- including research that is not relevant

- failing to explain the significance/meaning of the research presented
- focusing on only one aspect of the plan at the expense of others
- making overoptimistic forecasts or unsubstantiated claims
- avoiding discussion of problems and weaknesses
- forgetting to check the figures
- framing the plan in a context that does not align with the culture of the business.

Managing internal communication

Internal communication is the imparting, sharing and exchanging of information and messages within an organisation, between managers and employees, and across functions and departments. This may be face-to-face or remote, written or spoken, and may be carried out by a range of methods, including presentations, briefings, meetings, conversations, teleconferences, email, letters, memos, discussions and debates.

Communication plays a crucial role in every aspect of an organisation's operations and activities. When internal communication channels work well, tasks can be carried out in an efficient and timely manner, and employees are informed and involved and feel more engaged, committed, and valued. In addition, relationships can flourish at all levels of the organisation, improving coordination and collaboration between bosses, peers and employees. The establishment and embedding of good communication practices within the culture of an organisation facilitates the free flow of information and ideas, and the successful dissemination of information. Communicating the organisation's vision, mission, values and strategy clearly and transparently will enable employees to see how their role fits within the wider goals of the business, thus aiding motivation and commitment to achieving organisational objectives.

From mass communications to one-on-one exchanges, internal communication takes place formally as well as informally. Increasingly, it is taking place virtually, with the growing globalisation of business and the rise of digital communication platforms including mobile telephony, videoconferencing, the internet and social media, which offer opportunities not open to previous generations of managers. Digital technology helps to ensure that everyone is kept in touch at all times, irrespective of organisation size or structure. Digital media transcend geographical boundaries, so that those working remotely are never out of touch. If all communications are circulated swiftly, and all out-of-date information is promptly removed, everyone has full knowledge of how the organisation stands today rather than yesterday.

This checklist highlights factors which managers should take into consideration when seeking to ensure effective internal communications across an organisation, including the planning and delivery of individual messages.

Action checklist

1　Review internal communication frameworks and processes

Conduct a review of how employees are currently receiving and sharing information and how effectively communication channels are being used. Consider undertaking a full communication audit looking at information and communication needs – what needs to be communicated to whom and what are the best methods for doing so.

Ask yourself:

- Which channels are being used for different types of communications?
- How effectively is information being shared?
- Are key messages being communicated consistently across the organisation?
- What internal communication processes and procedures are in place?

- Are some employees fully informed and up-to-date, while others are left in the dark about what is happening in the organisation? How well they are performing?

- When changes are introduced, are all those who need to know about them informed in a timely manner?

- What procedures are in place to keep part-time and remote workers up-to-date, as well as those who are temporarily absent, on leave or away on business?

- What channels and technologies are being used?

- How can employees be involved in providing feedback on what works and what does not work for them?

- How can constructive ideas on improving communications be prompted and gathered from others?

2 Select the right delivery channels

Consider the pros and cons of different communication channels and how to use them appropriately:

- Face-to-face – all-staff briefings, team or departmental meetings and briefings, one-to-ones, presentations, workshops, focus groups, team away days

- Remote audio – telephone calls, conference calls, videoconferencing

- Paper-based – newsletters, memos, bulletins, letters, reports, posters, flyers, brochures

- Online – email, internet, intranets, social media, collaborative working tools.

Which channels you use will depend on a range of factors, including:

- the size and location of the organisation – whether it is single-site, multi-site or international

- whether all or some of the employees are office-based or work remotely

- the nature of the information to be communicated
- the timescale within which it needs to be delivered
- who – which individuals, groups and departments need to be informed
- costs – consider not just direct costs such as design or print but also indirect costs including time, venue and travel.

For example, all staff need to be publicly informed of a change in strategic direction, or a restructuring initiative, ideally at the same time, so an all-staff briefing or presentation may be appropriate. Alternatively, you might wish to cascade the information through senior managers to line managers and their teams. Changes affecting specific individuals will need to be communicated individually, preferably face-to-face and/or by letter. In many cases, using a combination of two or three channels will increase the effectiveness of a communication, as it will cater for individual preferences and ensure that the message is heard loud and clear by everyone.

If you opt for a verbal method of communication, such as a team meeting or presentation, provide briefing notes for the speakers, allowing for some personalisation but ensuring that all the relevant information is covered in a consistent manner. This gives managers the opportunity to clarify and make sense of the message before they broadcast the information to their teams. Supporting documents posted on the intranet or sent out by email will reinforce the message and ensure that those who work remotely or are unable to be present are fully aware of the situation. If you choose to use more than one method of communication, take care to make the message consistent so that there is no room for misunderstanding.

3 Ensure consistent communication processes and procedures

Putting standard processes in place and making sure that everyone in the organisation is aware of them will help to ensure effective and consistent communication. Decide how different types and levels of communication should be handled and draw up a framework that can be followed by all. For example, how will the following be carried out: updates on organisational performance and progress towards objectives; reports on successes and achievements; strategic adjustments or changes of direction; changes of personnel; major change initiatives; operational details; information on company policies and procedures? Consider also how new employees will be given access to the information they need to fulfil their job responsibilities and integrate into the organisation.

As well as procedures for top-down communication, standard processes should be implemented to enable employees to raise issues, ask questions and give feedback. Organisations often focus on cascading information downwards, so pay particular attention to ensuring that everyone knows how to communicate upwards, raising concerns and issues in a constructive way.

Employee surveys, opinion polls, formal interviews, questionnaires and suggestion schemes are just some of the ways to give employees the opportunity to share their views. Performance management programmes and performance appraisals should also provide an opportunity for employees to ask questions and discuss any problems they may have encountered. Adopt communication practices that are consistent with your organisation's style and culture to maximise engagement.

4 Be aware of your legal responsibilities

Although much of what is communicated internally will differ from one organisation to another, there are instances where all employers have a legal obligation to communicate with and consult the workforce. Depending on which national and international legislation applies, this may include areas such as health and safety, restructuring and redundancy. In the UK, the Information and Consultation of Employees Regulations (ICE) 2004 require organisations with more than fifty employees to put formal consultation procedures in place when sufficient members of the workforce request it, and larger employers must establish a European Works Council if sufficient employees request it.

5 Communicate the mission, vision, values and strategy of the organisation

All employees need to know what the organisation is trying to achieve and how it plans to do it. They need to understand how their own jobs and those of their colleagues, bosses and peers contribute to that mission and strategy. Corporate values also need to be communicated and integrated into individual attitudes and behaviour or they will be worthless. Think up creative ways to communicate organisational mission, vision and strategy – both long and short term – that are accessible to all employees.

6 Communicate change

Communication is a crucial part of any major change programme, and detailed communication plans should be drawn up for such initiatives. But small changes also need to be communicated, especially if they affect how people work. Make sure that changes are communicated clearly and openly early on in the process, so that any concerns or fears can be identified and reassurances given. Remember to explain the rationale for change, as well as the specifics of what will change and who will be responsible. Help people to make sense of new information by relating it to what they already know: the organisational mission or the current strategy, for example. Make sure your communications are rooted in context and convey a clear sense of why and how this is relevant to employees at this point in time.

7 Communicate business performance

To ensure that employees are engaged and informed, it is important to keep them informed about the performance and growth (or otherwise) of the organisation. Employees should be aware of how the organisation is performing, which targets are being met and where there are shortfalls. Most employees may not need or wish to see detailed financial reports, so provide summaries that give a good overview. Case studies or examples can also be used to bring the big picture to life, especially those that illustrate how organisational values and vision are being applied in real life by real people.

Do not cherry-pick particular aspects of financial performance to disclose. Be open and transparent, reporting both good and bad news, to avoid any nasty surprises later if performance fails to meet expectations. Unexpected bad news can cause the workforce to feel vulnerable, but if employees are fully aware of the situation they will be better prepared for any negative outcomes. Keeping employees in the dark is likely to raise suspicions and breed rumours and feelings of insecurity. It can also lead to managers being seen as secretive, dishonest and untrustworthy, so be open and gain the trust and support of your workforce.

8 Plan ahead

An organisational framework outlining procedures and processes to be followed should provide a sound foundation for routine communications. But it is still important to plan ahead, particularly when announcing big changes or introducing new initiatives. First establish the what, why, how, who and when:

- What do you want to say? What is the purpose of the message? What outcome do you hope to achieve?
- Why do you need to communicate this message?
- How will you communicate? What method(s) will you use?
- Who is your target audience? How are they likely to respond?
- When is the best time to deliver the message? Is it urgent? Is it a one-off announcement or will a communication programme be needed?
- How will you know if the communication is successful? What signs will indicate that it isn't working?

The answers will provide the basis for planning the delivery of the message or messages. Do not assume that when a message has been delivered once, it has been understood and taken on board by everyone. A series of repetitions and reminders, maybe presenting the information in a slightly different way, will maximise the retention and assimilation of the message. Some messages will need to be repeated at regular intervals. Examples would be reminders on subjects such as benefits available to employees, security policies or social-media usage guidelines. Organisational values also need to be revisited regularly.

9 Always keep your audience in mind

Your audience needs to be uppermost in your mind when devising and delivering internal messages. Stakeholder analysis could help you think about different groups within the organisation and their particular interests and information needs. This will enable you to tailor communications to avoid overwhelming some people with lots of information that is barely relevant to them or failing to inform others of matters with implications for their day-to-day working practices.

In general, think about who you are addressing: your boss, your employees, or your peers. Organisational hierarchy and culture, as well as the strength of the relationship you have with the recipients, will govern how formal, or otherwise, you can be and whether it is appropriate to impart your own opinions freely. Also take into account how much they already know (and how much they need to know).

Assess whether your audience will understand the use of abbreviations and acronyms or technical language. Consider the best means of engaging and reaching those you are addressing. If you are already aware that they favour one communication channel over another, be sure to use it, even if it is not your preferred method. Be sure, also, to take into account the needs of any employees with disabilities when planning your communications.

If your message is urgent, think carefully about the best means for delivering it. If you know that the intended recipient never replies to emails or has a stack of company newsletters sitting in their in-tray, you should avoid these channels and contact them in a more direct way. Use any existing knowledge of your audience to gauge their reaction to your communication and be ready with a response.

Consider the geographical location of your audience. If they are dispersed across different sites, think about how this will affect your ability to deliver the message consistently to all at the same time. This is particularly important if you have colleagues based overseas in different time zones. If you are aware that colleagues come from different cultural backgrounds, or that their first language differs from that used in the business, avoid using irony, jargon and humour that may cause offence in some contexts, or result in your message being lost in translation. Get to know your audience so you can always be certain your message will be received and understood.

10 Take advantage of social media

Social media is a valuable tool for communicating informal information across the organisation and enabling employees to share their opinions. It encompasses a range of different platforms including: wikis, blogs, discussion forums, RSS feeds, podcasts, video and intranet TV. Such tools can effectively encourage engagement and collaboration, as well as providing an instant way of sharing information and ideas. The creation of user-generated content provides opportunities to foster innovation and monitor the evolution of ideas and discussions. Social media can prove invaluable for making urgent announcements. However, be aware that not all of your intended audience will be accessing the information immediately.

Communicating online is largely 'faceless', which often gives individuals the confidence to express opinions that they may shy away from in face-to-face communication; this can have positive or negative results, which will need to be carefully managed. Your organisational guidelines should outline what kind of communications are appropriate online, but a supporting acceptable-use policy for social media should help to ensure that everyone abides by the same rules. Circulate this to all so that no one is in any doubt as to when social media can be used. Just as announcements can be made instantly, so too can feedback, so be sure to monitor your chosen platform regularly for any responses and provide feedback promptly.

The successful use of social media within an organisation relies on the technology supporting it. A lack of or out-of-date equipment, or poor broadband connectivity, will limit the value of this modern medium. So before adopting it as a communication platform, make sure that your organisation is fully set up to maximise its potential. Take into account the resource implications when introducing its use and weigh the cost of equipment, IT support and employee training against the potential return on investment. Be particularly mindful of the resources available to any overseas or remote colleagues.

11 Disseminate information accurately

If you are tasked with passing on a message to your own team or to a colleague (from your director or head of department, for example), be sure to do this accurately. Personal feelings, opinions and bias can distort a message and lead to the circulation of inaccurate or misleading information. Use direct quotes if necessary, especially if you find the message difficult to express. There are times when it is essential to repeat messages verbatim, especially if specific data such as annual turnover figures or number of job losses are involved. It is your responsibility to disseminate the message accurately. If you do not fully understand the message and/or its implications yourself, consult the briefing documents provided or seek clarification from the originator before trying to pass it on.

Similarly, if you want to convey a message to others through a third party such as your secretary or PA, make sure that they understand the message and interpret it correctly. For written communications, ask to see the final version before giving your consent for it to be circulated. Whether acting as the instigator or simply the messenger, you need to ensure that all internal communications are clear and transparent so that they will be effective and achieve the desired outcomes.

12 Evaluate internal communication practices

Review the effectiveness of internal communications regularly.

Ask questions such as:

- Are messages reaching the intended audiences?
- How well informed are employees?
- Are the right communication channels being used?
- Are there any new patterns emerging that necessitate changes to processes and procedures?
- How engaged are employees?
- Have there been any changes in attitudes or behaviour?
- Are communications too frequent or not frequent enough?
- Are the right resources such as technology and training plans in place?

Employee surveys and opinion polls are proactive ways of assessing how well, or otherwise, internal communication is received, understood and acted upon. One-to-one meetings, interviews and informal conversations also provide insight into how well internal communication is working. Allow time and opportunity for mass communications to be discussed in smaller groups or one-to-one, so that their impact can be more accurately assessed. Take all feedback and comments into account and take appropriate action.

As a manager you should avoid:

- using inappropriate communication channels

- ignoring established communication processes
- overloading communications with irrelevant information
- failing to evaluate communication practices
- failing to acknowledge the value of feedback from colleagues, and failing to use it to improve processes
- ignoring the benefits of social media.

Communicating across cultures

Cross-cultural communication is communicating with people whose ethnic and cultural backgrounds differ from your own.

With an increasingly multicultural working environment and a rise in global business opportunities, the ability to communicate with people from diverse ethnic and cultural backgrounds is an important managerial skill. Effective communication is essential in day-to-day business operations, whether managing employees, negotiating, networking, influencing or decision-making. If you do not possess the skills, or the confidence, to engage with people from different cultural backgrounds, you run the risk of damaging working relationships with colleagues and business partners and are likely to miss out on valuable opportunities that your competitors may be better equipped to handle.

Mastering the art of successful cross-cultural communication offers unique opportunities to open yourself up to new experiences, widen your social contacts and drive your business forward. Learning more about how colleagues, clients and suppliers from different cultural backgrounds think and behave, and the expectations they are likely to have, will enable you to build and strengthen existing relationships as well as form new ones. Although there are many pitfalls in cross-cultural communication, a genuine desire to treat individuals with respect, equity and integrity will form a firm foundation for building strong working relationships and communicating effectively with colleagues and business partners.

Cross-cultural communication relates to all types of internal and external exchange. It encompasses communicating with colleagues from different cultural backgrounds in your own workplace or organisation as well as with clients, customers and suppliers. Cross-cultural communication may take place face-to-face, remotely, or when travelling abroad on business. At times, it may involve communicating with people with a limited knowledge of the language in which business is being conducted. It is not concerned solely with communicating with those whose native tongue is different from your own, as communication barriers may exist between those who speak the same language. For example, divergent regional dialects, colloquialisms, and variances in spelling, expressions, humour, attitudes, behaviour and values often hinder comprehension or give rise to misunderstandings.

This checklist provides general guidance when communicating with individuals or groups in a cross-cultural context, both at home and abroad.

Action checklist

1 Improve your awareness and understanding of cultural diversity

Attitudes, values, beliefs and behaviour vary from one culture to another. What you may deem perfectly acceptable in your own society may be extremely offensive in another. For example, respect for hierarchy and authority and attitudes to gender, age and race are not consistent across every culture. In addition, attitudes to blame or shame, ways of expressing disagreement or discord, and approaches to punctuality and deadlines are areas where differences commonly occur.

An awareness of cultural differences can help managers to gauge how colleagues from differing background may respond to different types of communication and assist them in communicating effectively with them. Based on his international studies of IBM in the 1960s and 1970s, Geert Hofstede, a social psychologist, identified five distinct dimensions of cultural difference, covering issues such as levels of respect for authority, respect for individual freedom, acceptance of risk and uncertainty, and long-term or short-term orientation. His model provides a tool for raising awareness of cultural differences, but it is also important to understand that cultural norms vary across nations and are continuously evolving.

2 Beware of cultural stereotypes

An understanding of cultural differences is helpful, but avoid falling prey to cultural stereotypes that may be exaggerated, inaccurate or outdated. All nations are stereotyped to some extent and this affects how they are perceived by others, but generalising about an entire population could mean that you fail to truly understand the beliefs, attitudes, values and behaviour of an individual or group you have direct dealings with. Question any previously held assumptions, be open to learning from experience and base your judgements on your dealings with real people rather than on cultural stereotyping. Bear in mind that employees whose families have migrated to another country in the past or who have married into a different social group may appear to be fully integrated in their new society, but may have retained, to varying degrees, the behavioural norms of their cultural background.

3 Assess the situation within your organisation

When considering cross-cultural communications it is important to start by assessing the situation within your own organisation. For example, how diverse is the workforce you are tasked with managing? Are your teams based locally or in different regions or countries? Do you work with colleagues or business partners whose first language differs from your own or from the language in which business is conducted? What is the demographic of your client or supplier base? Are particular cultures and/or backgrounds strongly represented in your line of business? If you travel overseas for work, what are the implications of this in terms of your own communication skills?

If you identify any gaps in cultural understanding or language skills in yourself or your colleagues, consider how this could be addressed. A formal course of training may be necessary, or a more informal approach such as a buddy system may be helpful.

4 Adopt a flexible management style

Set realistic expectations about how you want to work and communicate with your own team, and how you plan to overcome any cultural or language barriers. You may need to adapt your leadership style to suit that of a cross-cultural team. Your age, race or gender may cause some team members to respond to your authority in a way you are not accustomed to, so think of ways to gain respect that all parties are comfortable with. The key is to work out why others react to you as they do and how you can overcome any barriers to leadership this may cause. You may need to think about how you can set expectations of 'how things are done around here' and how you will interact with those reporting to you. Depending on the diversity of your workforce, it may be necessary to adopt different managerial styles to handle those within your team from different cultures if a one-size-fits-all approach proves untenable.

5 Learn about the culture of others

Base your approach to different cultures on sensitivity, dignity and respect. Learn what you can about the cultures of others by observing and listening, and endeavour to gain a deeper understanding of values and behaviour. Watch how your colleagues interact with others from their own cultural background, as well as with those from a different one. See which methods of communication they favour, how they approach certain subjects and how they respond to different styles of communication. Reflect on how they approach social relationships and how they choose to communicate with different demographics. Observation will help you discern the most appropriate ways of conversing with people, enabling you to discover the most favourable way to gain positive responses to your communications and develop trust in your working relationships.

When meeting new colleagues or clients, and especially when travelling abroad on business, try to find out about the culture and customs in advance. If, for example, you are given an overseas assignment or will be visiting a particular region or country regularly, it may be possible to undertake a familiarisation course. This will provide an understanding to help you communicate effectively and build relationships. However, cross-cultural communication is not merely about watching and mimicry; it also involves a deeper understanding of different norms and values and an approach based on sensitivity, dignity and respect.

6 Choose the right communication channel and approach

There are many different communication channels, ranging from traditional print-based methods to the modern digital technologies. As far as circumstances allow, use what you have learned from previous observation to select a communication method that will be well received. Some managers may adopt a more informal, friendly approach as a means of building good working relationships, but employees from different backgrounds who have a strong respect for authority and hierarchy may find such an approach disrespectful. Similarly, in some cultures face-to-face communication is perceived as a sign of respect. So before settling on a casual email, tweet or blog, make sure that this will be well received. If in doubt, stick to a formal business approach initially, and, if possible, arrange a face-to-face meeting to gauge preferred cultural practices.

When approaching your communications, remember to take practical issues into consideration too. If you need to communicate with colleagues, customers or suppliers based overseas, consider what will work best for them, taking time zones and differentials into account. Think about the content and context of your message as well. Is it conducive to being shared in an informal way, or would a more structured, professional approach be appropriate?

7 Arrange appropriate times and/or places to communicate

When making arrangements for a meeting, either physical or virtual, you must avoid any times that are unsuitable. For example, religious holidays, prayer times, siestas/working hours abroad and general time differences can all play a part in making certain times of the day, week or year problematic for certain people. Being aware of religious holidays or times of worship demonstrates respect for other people's commitments and beliefs. Be willing to adapt and be flexible in order to meet the needs of others.

Where time differences are concerned, make sure you know whose time you are working to. If you are calling the meeting, make it clear which time zone it is in and use a twenty-four-hour clock to avoid confusion. If you are responding to a meeting request from someone overseas, make sure you know the time equivalent at home so the meeting is not inadvertently missed.

Choose appropriate venues for face-to-face meetings. People from some cultures like to do business in a social setting with food and drink, and some people fast at certain times of year and/or prohibit certain food and alcoholic drinks. If you are planning a face-to-face meeting and are concerned about attendees' lack of language skills, make things easier for all concerned by avoiding noisy locations or places where it is easy to be distracted by external activities.

8 Set expectations

You may be able to adjust your management style and take a flexible approach when dealing with individuals, but this may not be easy in multicultural contexts. In practice, most people accept that business meetings are carried out in line with the business culture of the host organisation, as long as respect is shown for individuals and their cultural sensitivities. In such circumstances, make sure that all attendees are aware of the framework to be used for the conduct of meetings and what will be expected of them.

9 Take care with non-verbal communication

Although body language can be helpful when emphasising a point, using inappropriate gestures could result in you inadvertently making a bad impression. Gestures that may be considered acceptable in one culture may be deemed highly offensive in another. Examples include physical contact such as embracing, kissing or shaking hands, pointing, and making direct eye contact. So do your homework to avoid making any social blunders. Take your lead from others to help you gauge what actions are acceptable. And remember to dress in an appropriate manner, as some forms of attire are frowned upon in certain cultures.

To prevent misunderstandings, make sure that your stance and body language match what you are saying. Your audience will gain confidence that they have understood your words by observing your body language, so this will reinforce your message. Be aware, too, that body language and the tone, pitch, inflection and volume of your voice also play a large part in communication, even if the words are not fully understood.

10 Take care with foreign languages

To maximise the impact of your communications, ascertain how much of the language used for business in your organisation your audience actually understands. Being able to handle a casual exchange of pleasantries confidently does not necessarily mean that someone possesses the vocabulary or language skills to understand a complex business matter. Bear in mind that your audience may be more adept at speaking than writing or reading, or vice versa. Having an awareness of this will not only help you select the most appropriate method of communication; it will also determine how successful your communication is likely to be.

Do not patronise your audience by speaking excessively slowly or in a loud voice. This is likely to make listeners feel uncomfortable and undermine their position. Be patient and be prepared to dedicate time to helping them comprehend you better. Cultural norms may lead people to smile and nod their understanding out of politeness. This can deceive you into thinking that they have understood more than they may have. Ask pertinent questions to assess how much has been understood and to clarify meaning if you are not sure you have understood others correctly. Enlist the services of a translator or an interpreter if necessary. However, be aware of the inherent risks of bias in translation and of potential difficulties in finding exact translations for certain words and concepts. Both can compromise meaning and comprehension. An error in a single word can lead to huge misunderstandings if care is not taken to check the intended meaning.

11 Choose your language carefully

Using appropriate language will help you deliver your message clearly and concisely. Keep to the point. The use of flowery language, superfluous descriptive words, idiomatic expressions or numerous asides can baffle someone whose understanding of the language being used is less than perfect. Likewise, steer clear of jargon, acronyms or technical language unless you are certain your audience will understand them. Try to avoid words that have more than one meaning. Even when conversing with others with the same native language, regional dialects and colloquialisms can get lost in translation. Humour is easily misunderstood, so avoid it. The same applies to irony and sarcasm. Repeat important words or phrases to emphasise a point and keep messages short and simple so that they are more likely to be understood and remembered by the audience.

Learning a few basic words or phrases in the native language of those you wish to communicate with will do much to strengthen relationships between you. This is especially important if you are travelling to another country on business where English is not the native language. Assuming that everyone speaks fluent English and that you do not need to make an effort will do little to make a good first impression or gain the favour of those you are meeting. Being prepared to learn a few words of the host country's language demonstrates your respect for another culture and shows that you are keen to make a good impression. Similarly, if you are hosting an overseas visitor in the UK, it is considerate to learn a few words of greeting in their native tongue. This will act as an icebreaker and your thoughtfulness will help to make the visitor feel at home in your country.

However well prepared you are, misunderstandings are bound to occur when there are language barriers. Be on the alert for any problems of this kind and act at once to resolve them. How you handle such misunderstandings will affect how you and your company are perceived by the other party and help to repair any damage to relationships.

12 Be aware of listening habits

People from different cultures may not listen and respond in the same way. Your audience may listen attentively, giving you their undivided attention. Conversely, they may become easily distracted, be impatient to hear what you have to say, or rudely interrupt you before you have finished speaking. People from some cultures are renowned for listening politely, while others are known for voicing their opinions loud and clear. Having an awareness of your audience's likely response to your communications will aid you in planning the most appropriate approach to take, and in anticipating how much, or little, feedback and interaction you can expect. If possible, observe the reaction of your audience to presentations and communications delivered by others before planning your own.

As a manager you should avoid:

- making cultural assumptions based on stereotypes
- forgetting to check that your communication has been clearly understood

- using inappropriate non-verbal communication gestures
- adopting an inflexible management style
- being ignorant or disrespectful of other people's cultures.

Communicating in the virtual workplace

A virtual workforce consists of employees (or an employee) who are in a different physical location from their manager, or are dispersed in a number of different locations. This may be those working in different parts of a single building or site, but more commonly it is those who work from home for some or all of their working hours, mobile workers operating in the field, those working in outsourced teams, or those working at a different site, either within the same country or abroad.

In today's world of international business, flexible working practices and cutting-edge technologies, virtual working is common in organisations across the world. The benefits of virtual working are many and varied, for both the organisation and the employees. Yet remote working does have its challenges.

For managers responsible for overseeing employees at a different site, in a different region, or even in a different country from their own, there are various issues to be addressed. Communication is a crucial element, and it is important to get it right. Managing from a distance requires a different approach to communications, with an emphasis on clarity and transparency.

In a physical working environment, much of what we learn from our colleagues is gained through observation. We see how they work and get a sense of their attitudes and expectations and the meaning of what they say through facial expressions and body language. However, such visual clues are not available to colleagues who work remotely. For this reason it is essential for managers to set clear expectations and to pay attention to communicating organisational values, goals and culture as well as everyday messages and information. Getting messages of this type across to colleagues whom they may never have met in person is a challenge that managers need to find ways to overcome.

The absence of physical managerial contact when team members are remote or dispersed makes the development of trust even more important if objectives are to be achieved and targets met. As well as being an effective communicator, a virtual manager needs to be adept at collaborating with and coordinating the team so as to develop those all-important trusting relationships. This checklist provides pointers for managing a virtual workforce with a particular focus on clear communication.

Action checklist

1 Establish the dynamics of your workforce

In order to adopt the most effective means of communicating and to tailor your approach according to the context, the first step is to consider the dynamics of your team and to identify what the specific needs of team members may be. Virtual working covers a range of different scenarios and working environments, so the needs of your team members will be varied and complex. Those who have no direct face-to-face exchanges will encounter different challenges from those who have occasional contact. These can range from poor IT or communication skills, cultural or language barriers, difficulties of location and time, identity issues and feelings of isolation. All such concerns need to be assessed and addressed one-to-one. Be aware that one solution may not suit all your team members, even those who are facing similar challenges, and try to find ways of meeting individual needs. Where skills gaps are identified, take a proactive approach to provide informal or formal training.

The team dynamic can be fragile. Relationships among team

members take longer to establish when colleagues rarely, if ever, see or speak to each other in person. A new employee joining the team or someone leaving can have a much greater impact than when it occurs in a physical workplace. So be patient and be prepared to allow time to rebuild your team once the balance has been disturbed.

2 Understand the working environment

As a manager, it is important to be aware that the environment in which your employees work may be very different from your own. Location has a significant bearing on your ability to communicate with colleagues effectively and frequently. If they are based overseas, there will be language barriers and time differences, as well as connection costs and the availability of technology. If employees are operating on the move, from a car, train or plane, for example, your choice of communication method and the timing of your messages will be affected. If your team members are mobile, you need to reach an agreement on how you will know when they are available and how you can get hold of them when necessary.

When colleagues are in a public place where they can be overheard or interrupted this can cause difficulties, especially when you need to discuss personal or sensitive information. Background noise can also be a problem. Access to reliable technology, support and connections to phone and internet networks may be compromised if recipients are travelling around, or based in a location with poor connectivity. Being aware of these issues will enable you to put contingencies in place and avoid the frustration of being unable to contact a colleague when you need to.

3 Build the team and create a collaborative workforce

Relationships evolve organically when team members work side by side at the same physical location and, in time, with the help of a good leader, the team begin to bond and develop a sense of common purpose. Remote workers, however, may never come into contact with their colleagues, so you need to devise ways of bringing lone or dispersed workers together to communicate with each other as well as with you. Provide opportunities for the team to meet virtually to share ideas, opinions and progress reports. Ask workers to explain what their roles are and what they are currently working on.

Audio- and videoconferencing are effective ways of bringing a virtual team together and getting everyone to communicate. Seeing what someone looks like on a screen or even just hearing their voice can aid recognition and familiarity. Consider reinforcing this by circulating employees' photographs and contact details, if appropriate.

Make it clear that team members will have to communicate with each other to get the answers they need. Investigate the use of collaborative technologies such as shared databases, wikis, intranets and cloud-based work platforms to encourage the exchange of knowledge, information and ideas. By creating an environment conducive to group collaboration, you effectively give workers a group identity and a sense of belonging. Collaboration is achievable when everyone is working towards a shared goal, irrespective of their status, background or working environment. Collaborative working underpins good internal communication, so dedicate time to getting this right.

4 Reinforce organisational practices, values and behaviour

In a physical workplace, an understanding of organisational policies and practices covering such matters as etiquette, dress codes, acceptable and unacceptable behaviour, appropriate use of humour, and when and how to interact with senior members of staff can be gained by simply observing others. Newcomers quickly learn about an organisation's culture and politics in this way. However, virtual workers frequently lack such visible social clues to inform or prompt them. Electronic communications can also lend a degree of anonymity, which leads people to say things that would not be deemed appropriate in a face-to-face exchange.

It is therefore the responsibility of the manager to communicate the organisation's policies, values and accepted behaviour explicitly and to make sure that they are followed. There need to be set guidelines for acceptable behaviour so that people know what is expected of them. These should be clearly communicated, documented and acted upon by all concerned, so that organisational standards are met. Any deviation from or disregard of guidelines should be addressed promptly. Be clear about what you expect of your employees and what they can expect from you in return. Take every opportunity to reinforce the messages through your own behaviour – adopting the right form of address in emails, always arriving promptly for virtual meetings and showing respect for the opinions of others. Shared behaviour, values and policies help to create a collaborative and cohesive workforce with all members working to the same high standards.

5 Gain, build and maintain trust

It is crucial to gain, build and maintain trust with all your team members if they are to remain engaged and motivated at all times. Trust can take time to build, especially when you do not have the benefit of meeting face-to-face, so it is important to maintain regular contact. Employees need to know you are available to support them and deal with queries when necessary and that the distance between you is purely a physical one.

Avoid sending only group communications and make an effort to communicate with individual team members. Ask how they are, rather than making contact simply to check up on a task they have been set. Depending on the context, a casual email or exchange of pleasantries that is not solely about work can help to strengthen a trusting relationship.

Be as transparent as you can – in your communications, your expectations and your requirements. This will allow trust to develop and uncertainty to be eradicated. Managing from a distance limits your ability to exercise control, so you need to be in a position to trust your team members to keep on track and fulfil the responsibilities allocated to them. Show that you have confidence in their ability and trust them to work without constant supervision or control.

6 Provide, and seek, regular feedback

Be sure to provide regular feedback on the performance of each team member. A yearly appraisal may not be the most appropriate means of assessing and discussing the performance of a virtual worker. A year is too long, for problems go undetected and fester. Aim to give feedback and provide opportunities for workers to discuss their progress with you regularly.

As well as providing feedback on performance, it is important to keep track of progress and enable employees to make adjustments as necessary. Request regular progress updates as a means of managing the workflow and maintaining a degree of managerial control.

Give workers the opportunity to provide feedback on how projects are developing, choosing a suitable method of enabling them to do this. It can be helpful to set up an open forum, where team members can share ideas and discuss problems together, as well as a closed communication channel, where individuals can share sensitive or private information in confidence. Asking for the opinions of all the team members will do much to increase engagement and make lone workers feel more supported and less isolated.

Feedback is a two-way process, so it is important that you seek opinions from your employees as to how they feel they are being managed – the things that are working and not working from their perspective and what they need from you. Encouraging feedback will help you to identify any concerns, and to adapt your own practices and approach to better suit their needs.

7 Give recognition and reward where deserved

Motivation and engagement can be greatly enhanced by judicious use of recognition and reward, for both team projects and individual achievements. Consider the best way to reward your team members for a job well done. This might be a mention at an all-staff briefing, a dedicated piece in the company's newsletter or intranet pages, or a financial incentive for those working on commission, for example. Each organisation has its own formal methods of recognising and rewarding team and individual performance, but adopting a few informal means of commending people for a job well done will do much to strengthen your relationship with your team. Choose the most appropriate method to communicate achievements; being sure to credit individuals by name.

8 Monitor productivity regularly

Managing and monitoring the productivity of a virtual workforce can be a challenge. If every task you set has a month's deadline attached to it, it will be difficult to assess whether workers are productive all the time or are simply working round the clock a week before the deadline is due. Setting varied tasks and deadlines helps to keep workloads manageable for yourself as well as your team and ensures that you are constantly in touch with each other.

It is also important to recognise, and act upon, underperformance. Failure to meet targets, missed deadlines, absence, or late arrival at virtual meetings may indicate that an individual is struggling to cope with their workload or indeed has become disengaged. Both are serious issues which need to be dealt with promptly. Although many indicators of disquiet are obvious when you are working alongside a person – body language and tone of voice, for example – unease is harder to detect when you do not interact with your employees face-to-face. This is why regular contact is so important and why it is vital that connections are established and maintained. Building good working relationships and trust helps to ensure that you are kept in the picture at all times and can make allowances for circumstances that are beyond your team's control. If you have to deal with a serious matter, think about the best way to approach this and choose the time and channel of communication with care. Bear in mind that some forms of electronic communication are regarded as informal; in some cases adopting a more traditional means of communication, such as a letter, may be more appropriate.

9 Put in place the right technology and training

Virtual working and virtual management rely heavily on technology, including e-communication and social-media platforms. If communication is to be effective, you need to make sure that all technology and software in use are fully supported. Equipment needs to be up-to-date and fully operational; mobile phone reception and broadband connections should be available at acceptable levels; and all members of the team need to be able to access the same technology at the same time. Frustrating interruptions caused by technical faults or bandwidth problems can swiftly disrupt a virtual meeting. Be prepared by checking that everything is fully operational before a meeting and encouraging participants to do the same.

As well as having the right technology and IT support in place, it is also crucial for all employees to receive training to equip them with the skills they need. Be aware that remote workers may not have any IT support on-site or close by, especially if they operate from home, and try to make sure that no one in your team is at a disadvantage where technology is concerned. Ask your employees to complete an assessment questionnaire and/ or undertake a skills audit, so you can accurately assess who may need training or additional support. Make arrangements to meet any training needs you identify and ensure that the training is undertaken promptly. Similarly, any skill gaps in your own knowledge should be addressed.

10 Evaluate e-communication methods

There are a number of different technologies and software programmes for remote communication. When considering which are most appropriate for your use, think about the content and context of the information you want to deliver. Options include:

- telephone conferencing
- videoconferencing
- online meeting platforms
- discussion forums
- email
- social media
- intranets
- webinars.

Each method of communication has its own merits, as well as pitfalls, so consider them carefully before making a selection. Ask the following questions:

- How formal or informal does the communication need to be?
- How large or small is the group you are communicating with?
- Do you and your team possess the requisite technical knowledge and is the necessary equipment available?
- Do you require instant responses to a message?
- Are participation and interaction important?

In a physical working environment, these means of communication are often used as adjuncts to face-to-face communication. In a virtual one, the rules for using them change as they become the primary means of communicating. Think about how to adapt your use of these technologies and encourage co-workers to do likewise.

11 Ensure clear and detailed communication at all times

Whichever communication method you choose, remember that without visual clues, the need to communicate fully and clearly is paramount. It is easy for messages to be misunderstood and misinterpreted when communications are sparse. Communication needs to be clear and transparent, yet also much more detailed than might be necessary in a face-to-face exchange. Supplying additional or background information is therefore essential. You should also invite feedback explicitly, so that recipients know when to respond and when to listen. Be sure to give delegates the opportunity to seek clarification and ask questions – either during a virtual meeting or afterwards. When complex tasks are involved, take care to provide guidance notes to reinforce what has been communicated, discussed and agreed.

Additional challenges arise when communicating with colleagues whose native language or cultural background is not the same as your own. Language barriers can prevent your message from being understood, so you must be fully aware of the written and spoken language skills of everyone in your workforce. Levels of ability among your team may vary, so if you notice the same individuals doing all the talking in group meetings check that the silence of others is not on account of a lack of understanding. Test this by addressing direct questions to named individuals. Familiarise yourself with the cultural expectations of team members from varying backgrounds and do all you can to encourage interaction and participation.

As a manager you should avoid:

- ambiguous or infrequent communications
- assuming that everyone in the team has the same needs
- using inappropriate technologies
- failing to provide feedback on performance
- forgetting that virtual workers require instruction and guidance.

Claude Shannon
Father of information theory

Introduction

Claude Shannon (1916–2001) had considerable talents and interest in the disciplines of electrical circuitry, mathematics, cryptology and code breaking. His early work in these areas was to evolve into the concept of information theory, a discipline that he introduced in his seminal work, *A Mathematical Theory of Communication*, published in 1948. In it he details his theory of communication, an approach that was new and innovative. This pioneering publication laid the foundations for information theory and earned Shannon the title of founding father.

Shannon understood signal processing and its relationship to data storage, compression and transmission. Crucially, he approached information as a physical mass, deducing as a result that information can be measured. He proved that all communication, as diverse as radio waves, text, pictures and telephone signalling, can be programmed in binary numbers. Before his discovery, the different types of communication had been transmitted using entirely different media. This all-inclusive approach to communication was groundbreaking and effectively set Shannon apart from the crowd, making him one of the most significant early pioneers of the digital age we live in today.

Life and career

Born in Michigan in the US in 1916, Shannon demonstrated his talent for mechanics and electronics in his innovative childhood inventions. He continued to invent games and mechanical devices into his adulthood, indulging in his passion for games as well as his innate creativity. One such invention was an electromechanical mouse, which was his first foray into artificial intelligence. Another was a device for calculating casino odds. Frippery or fun, Shannon's 'playful' inventions left their mark.

As a young man, Shannon cemented his interests in academic study, graduating from the University of Michigan in 1936 with degrees in mathematics and electrical engineering. After the completion of his early studies, Shannon undertook a graduate degree in electrical engineering at the Massachusetts Institute of Technology (MIT), where he worked with early analogue computers as an assistant to Vannevar Bush, an early pioneer in this field.

His interest in the workings of circuit systems and mathematical relationships was developed further during his academic studies when he was exposed to the work of George Boole, of Boolean logic fame. This led the tenacious young Shannon to work out how Boole's logic could be applied to greater effect in relation to electrical switches, namely telephone call-routing switches. Although Shannon was not the first to develop Boolean logic in this way, it was only when he wrote about his findings in his thesis that it became widely known and accepted. Shannon's discovery effectively formed the basis of digital circuit design.

After the success and recognition of his early work, Shannon turned his considerable talents to cryptology, culminating in a venture into code breaking and designing secure telecommunications. Such cryptology and code-breaking prowess led Shannon to the discovery that the One-Time Pad, an encryption technique, is unbreakable. From his findings, he concluded that all codes must have the same requirements as the One-Time Pad system if they are to remain incorruptible. Although numerous people have been credited with an involvement in the development and use of the One-Time Pad since Frank Miller's first connection in 1882, Shannon was the first to demonstrate the theoretical implications of this encryption system as a totally secure model.

Many of Shannon's early achievements and explorations took place during the Second World War when he was involved in national defence while working at Bell Laboratories. It was at this time that he produced *A Mathematical Theory of Communication*.

In 1956 Shannon joined the faculty at MIT, where he remained until 1978.

Influences

Shannon was influenced by many of his predecessors and contemporaries, whose ideas he embraced and admired. As well as Boole and Bush, he was inspired by Harry Nyquist (pioneering work on telegraph speeds), Ralph Hartley (a researcher on repeaters, carrier and voice transmission) and Alan Turing (an eminent British cryptologist and mathematician).

Shannon expanded upon existing theories and discoveries and was the first person to consider communication as a statistical process, understanding as he did that information is measurable. This is what underpins information theory. Through their own work, fellow Bell Labs' employees Nyquist and Hartley undoubtedly helped Shannon lay the foundations of what was to become information theory. Although he was not always the originator of an idea, Shannon had the knowledge and talent to explore further the seeds of ideas dropped by others, probing a little deeper and researching more fully until he was confident that a developed theory could be proven and substantiated mathematically.

Key theories

Shannon's early insights into communication theory and cryptology during the Second World War cemented his passion in this field of research and led to the development of groundbreaking theories. His mathematical leanings are evident in his research, as he substantiated his ideas and logic with complex mathematical equations and formulas.

Shannon's discoveries in code breaking and communication theory were taken a step further as he attempted to discern how best to effectively programme the information the sender wants to broadcast so that the intended message is sent and understood. Recognising that doubt can arise in communication and lead to miscommunication, Shannon developed the notion of information entropy as a means of measuring such uncertainty and statistically gauging how much information is contained within a received message.

From his work in the field of information theory came several offshoot theories, such as channel capacity and noisy channel coding. Through his research, Shannon understood the upper limits of data transmission and compression before a message is effectively lost. Such limits are theorised in Shannon's source coding theorem. He also explored the limitations of communication when noise is present in relation to bandwidth, which is reflected in the Shannon–Hartley theorem.

Communication process model

Warren Weaver, a renowned scientist and pioneer of machine translation, helped popularise *A Mathematical Theory of Communication*, and together Shannon and Weaver developed the first model of the communication process. This model was originally developed for use in mechanical messaging for the Bell Telephone Company. Shannon and Weaver's model demonstrates what happens when we communicate. They illustrated communication exchange as a series of steps, which are roughly as follows:

- The communicator moves the information they wish to impart from their brain to their mouth (transmitting device) using appropriate words, which can be written or spoken.

- Once the words are imparted through the communication channel (voice, email, etc), the message is sent through the air towards the receiver, who decodes the message.

- Along the way, the message is joined by other sounds and distractions (noise) that can alter its meaning.

- The receiver decodes the message, reconstructing the meaning to minimise noise.

- The message is received and understood.

Shannon and Weaver's model effectively demonstrated what happens when we communicate with others. They highlighted the potential hazards the message encounters from transmission to receipt which can distort content and lead to miscommunication. They recognised that natural language processing can be compromised by interfering noise, which leads to communication failure. When the same message is transmitted using a combination of methods, such as verbal and digital, the potential for miscommunication increases.

By approaching the communication process as a series of steps, Shannon and Weaver made it possible to pinpoint where communication may fail. They showed unequivocally that a problem with encoding, channel, noise or decoding can result in the failure or breakdown of effective information transmission and retrieval.

In perspective

Shannon received countless awards and accolades, including numerous honorary doctorates, the National Medal of Science, awarded by President Lyndon Johnson in 1966, and a posthumous entry in the National Inventors' Hall of Fame in 2004.

Outside the sphere of technological and information experts,
Shannon's work remains largely unknown. Yet his contribution
and impact are immense. Through his work, Shannon effectively
introduced the information and computing fraternity to the
limitations, and possibilities, of data storage, compression and
transmission, paving the way for such inventions as CDs, DVDs,
MP3s and JPEGs, among others.

Shannon's work transformed telecommunications with the
move from analogue to digital transmission. His findings also
smoothed the way for understanding digital communications and
content messaging, so relevant today. His discoveries regarding
the ability to measure information content were the founding
principles in the measurement of digital transmissions as bits per
minute.

Such is the impact of Shannon's work that it can be argued
he helped to lay the foundations of the digital revolution of the
twenty-first century. The application of his work also extends
to other disciplines such as physics, statistics, economics and
psychology.

As for Shannon himself, he was uncomfortable being in the
spotlight. As information theory became the new buzzword of the
day, he gradually retreated from teaching and academic life. He
seemed surprised by the impact of and overwhelming response
to his work and ideas.

Brainstorming

Brainstorming is a technique for generating ideas, developing creativity, or solving problems in small groups through the free-flowing contributions of participants. Several variations of brainstorming and related techniques have emerged, such as brainwriting (where individuals write down ideas), nominal group technique, electronic brainstorming and buzz discussion groups.

The purpose of this checklist is to enable a manager, without previous experience of the technique and with a minimum of preparation, to introduce brainstorming to a group and then go on to brainstorm a specific problem or opportunity.

Brainstorming can generate numerous fresh ideas and novel approaches, and can be fun and easy to learn. Despite controversy over the effectiveness of brainstorming groups compared with individual efforts at problem solving, brainstorming has many supporters. The use of a well-trained facilitator can overcome most difficulties or limitations and achieve additional benefits, including enhanced member involvement and group interaction.

It is worth noting that to avoid offence to people with conditions such as epilepsy, alternative terms such as thought showers or cloud bursting may be adopted, but the term brainstorming is still widely used.

Action checklist: preparation

1 Select the problem or opportunity to be brainstormed

Select a topic important enough to justify the participation of others. This is likely to be something of particular importance to your organisation, perhaps a new product or strategic initiative. It should also be one with a number of possible solutions and where imagination and creative lateral thinking are required to identify these and assess their relative value.

2 Think about structure, aims and objectives

Although brainstorming sessions are usually thought of as open, no-holds-barred affairs, establishing where you are going, what you want to achieve and broadly how you hope to get there is likely to provide a helpful framework. Some brainstorming sessions place constraints on participants to help them to focus their minds, work more effectively and discover workable solutions. Whether or not you provide guidance and/or restrictions, it is important to consider how to phrase the original question or topic. A clear, thought-provoking question can make a real difference to the quality of responses from the brainstorming group.

3 Choose the facilitator

Choosing the right facilitator is crucial: the person should be open and outgoing, with enthusiasm and the ability to stimulate interest and enjoyment. The facilitator does not need to be the most senior person at the session, but they should set the scene by creating an open atmosphere, controlling dominant people while encouraging participation from the more introverted group members, getting and keeping participants on track by highlighting the issues, and creating a sense of fun. Perhaps most importantly, they should be adept at keeping ideas flowing and be able to go with the flow themselves.

Should the facilitator be internal or external? An external facilitator can be especially useful when senior managers are involved or where confidentiality is required. But if the issue is not too complex or contentious, an internal facilitator may be used, provided they have some experience.

The facilitator should feel comfortable running activity-based sessions, and should have clear plans and tactics for arriving at particular outcomes or targets. They must also ensure, as much as possible, that the group works as a team and takes ownership of the ideas it comes up with.

4 Select an appropriate venue

This depends largely on the time set aside for the session and the budget available. If possible, somewhere away from the workplace is often more suitable and can help to bring a fresh perspective to the business in hand. Depending on the length of the session, you may wish to provide refreshments at the venue – these can also act as an incentive to attend.

5 Consider the mix of participants

As well as people with a specialist contribution to make, include some who have little or no knowledge of the topic to be brainstormed. They will not be as familiar with the detail and will offer a fresh approach. For this reason consider introducing outsiders, although this can backfire if they are seen as intruders or spies. A mix of representatives from different cultural backgrounds could be valuable to provide a range of perspectives on the issues to be discussed. Work on getting the group dynamics right to put the group at ease, avoid snide comments or put-downs and create a blame-free atmosphere. All participants should be seen as equals, and treated as such.

6 Decide on the number of participants

There is no right number, although more than ten might be unmanageable when ideas really start to flow, and less than four might not be enough to generate creativity. A large group can also inhibit participation from quieter members, and allows those unwilling and unenthusiastic to avoid making a contribution. Four to eight is usually about right, although this will depend on the style of the facilitator and the nature of the issue to be tackled.

7 Get the equipment right

You will need some method of recording the ideas that come up. Audio and video recording may seem to be ideal for this, but participants can find these devices off-putting and recording can inhibit the free flow of ideas. A flip chart and a plentiful supply of felt-tip pens are often adequate, with completed sheets attached to the wall in full view to help stimulate further ideas. Consider also using technology such as laptops and projectors or interactive whiteboards, but make sure that all participants are clear on how to use the technology before the session starts.

8 Get the layout right

Do not use a room with fixed rows of seats. Something more relaxed, even random, is preferable; a circle or U-shape is usual. The facilitator should check the room beforehand and prepare it appropriately.

9 Get the timing right

Reflect on your own powers of concentration and remember that in brainstorming sessions people can move from being dynamically engaged to feeling exhausted and back again. Ten to twenty minutes may be needed to get people relaxed. However, two hours can be a long time to brainstorm, so stop for a while if people show signs of tiredness. Arrange for a twenty-minute break after an hour's uninterrupted flow, or if and when the flow slows to a trickle. The break may be enough to stimulate an active restart, perhaps with a change in the seating of individuals.

10 Get the time of day right

Unfortunately, it is difficult to give hard and fast advice on timing, as people differ. Some will function better after their routine work has been completed, when their minds are less preoccupied and they feel they can be more relaxed; others may prefer the morning when collective mental energy is at its highest.

11 Consider the role of pre-session brainstorming

Although brainstorming is often perceived as a spontaneous activity, you should provide sufficient notice of the session and, if possible, an outline of the problem to be tackled. This approach is likely to help those group members who like to have time to think through an idea and find it difficult to think on their feet.

You may also wish to ask participants to submit some initial ideas before the session begins. This can be done easily and anonymously using cloud-computing technologies such as Google Drive. As well as being a preferred method of communication for introverts, doing this may help get the ball rolling at the official brainstorming session.

Action checklist: the session

1 State the topic or opportunity to be explored

State the topic and explain it to the group. Make sure everyone participating has a clear understanding of the issue and the objectives of the session. Ask participants if they have any initial questions and encourage them to behave in a courteous and constructive manner towards one another.

2 Restate the situation

Encourage the group to stand back from the topic, walk around it and see it from every angle. Suggest rewording it in 'How to' statements. Some restatements may be close to the original; others may illuminate new facets. Display these new statements on flip charts, projectors or whiteboards for everyone to see.

3 Brainstorm the problem with these guidelines

- Suspend judgement. Avoid negative evaluative comments such as 'That won't work' or 'That sounds silly'. Laugh with wild ideas, not at them.

- Accept that there may be a level of cynicism and lack of enthusiasm among participants. Bets, competitions and prizes can be used to counteract this.

- Consider using the following to generate further ideas:
  - call for a one-minute break, asking the group to look over ideas already noted before starting the flow again
  - offer a target, such as 'We just need six more to make fifty ideas!'
  - reflect and concentrate on one idea, such as 'How many ways are there to do this?'
  - look back at the restatements to pursue other lines of inquiry.

- Freewheel. Encourage (within limits) drifting or dreaming, and try to bring the subconscious into play. The wilder the idea, the better.

- Go for quantity not quality. The more the merrier; suspend judgement for the time being. Evaluation will come later.

- Cross-fertilise. Pick up someone else's idea and suggest others leading from it.

- Encourage group members to choose a really wild and apparently senseless idea from the lists they have made and generate ideas based on or arising from it.

4 Closure

Give a warning about five minutes from the end of the session. Participants will want to know what happens next. Explain that the lists will be circulated and do this within twenty-four hours, if possible, to retain freshness and familiarity. Provide contact details or a way of submitting additional ideas or further background information after the session and set a deadline for doing this. You may find that some participants have their best ideas after the session, when they have had time to think about it.

Inform participants that they will be notified of the ideas chosen or recommended for further action. Ask one last time for any comments, ideas or further thinking and thank members of the group for their participation.

Action checklist: evaluation

1 Get the group to scrutinise all the ideas and pick out any instant winners

Rank ideas giving three points for those that stand out, two for those that have possibilities and one for those that appear unsound, require too many resources, or do not meet the original objectives.

2 Reduce the number of twos to a minimum

To reduce the number of ideas rated two, apply criteria such as cost and acceptability, and consider whether the timescale is appropriate.

3 Apply reverse brainstorming to the ideas

- In how many ways can a particular idea fail?
- What are the negative factors?
- What is the potential downside for the organisation?

4 Apply the key evaluative criteria

- What will it cost?
- Will it be acceptable to management, staff and customers?
- Is it legal?
- Is it practical?
- How long will it take?
- How easy will it be to implement?
- What competition will there be?

● How time-sensitive or urgent is it? (If it is not done now, will an opportunity be lost?)

The main brainstorming session should be free of negativity, but there is a need for critique and evaluation at this stage to make the session constructive and useful. Brainstorming should ultimately provide solutions that are both original and workable, rather than a stream of unfeasible suggestions.

As a manager you should avoid:

● allowing unconstructive critical comments
● letting the session be dictated or sidetracked by dominant individuals
● letting the session go on too long
● recording the whole session
● allowing the session to be used to get buy-in for an existing idea.

Public relations planning

The UK Chartered Institute of Public Relations defines public relations practice as follows:

Public relations is about reputation – the result of what you do, what you say and what others say about you.

Public relations is the discipline that looks after an organisation's reputation. Its aim is to win understanding and support and influence opinion and behaviour. It establishes and maintains goodwill and mutual understanding between an organisation and its publics.

Media relations is an integral aspect of public relations, and involvement in online and social-media communication and brand management is important in securing the right profile in the press, on radio and television and online. Public relations planning as a whole, however, should focus more broadly on engaging with all stakeholder groups. It involves focusing on the overall business aims and objectives of your organisation and developing public relations objectives that will support these and link to the overall business plan.

Public relations (PR) can be a powerful force in promoting and enhancing organisational reputation. It has been suggested that getting others to say something positive about you has a much greater impact than saying it yourself. Although PR has traditionally been seen as secondary to marketing and advertising efforts, the advent of social media has hugely increased its importance. The development of social-media platforms has opened up a plethora of relatively low-cost opportunities for organisations to communicate and interact directly with their public and audiences, including customers, consumers and activists. Satisfied and dissatisfied customers can provide instant feedback and suggestions which are rapidly communicated to a wide online audience. Media organisations are looking for engaging content which will drive traffic to their websites, providing opportunities for organisations to provide relevant and engaging information for public consumption. Indeed, PR campaigns are increasingly reliant on their ability to create content that people will want to share and talk about online.

Conversely, poor handling of PR both online and offline can have a hugely detrimental effect on a business and its ability to maintain competitive advantage and profitability. Paying due attention to PR enables managers to handle the reputation of their organisation and influence how it is perceived externally by stakeholders, rather than leaving it to chance. Taking the trouble to develop the right skills and knowledge helps managers to avoid PR blunders that could damage the reputation and sustainability of their organisation. In short, managing PR effectively can:

- improve an organisation's reputation
- enhance corporate image
- create awareness of a product or service or brand, leading to a growth in sales
- generate support for an organisation's work
- develop long-term business relationships
- improve staff recruitment, retention and engagement.

This checklist is designed to help those with little or no background in PR to begin to manage this area effectively within their organisation. It provides a model for developing a public relations plan that supports the organisation's overall aims and objectives and gives guidance on press and PR activities. It is designed for use by managers in all sectors and in any type of organisation.

Action checklist

1 Define target stakeholders

The stakeholder groups you need to communicate with will depend on the nature of your business, but they can be broadly defined as:

- customers/clients – those who buy or use your products or services
- the media – press, radio, TV (terrestrial and satellite), online news publishers, social-media platforms
- internal groups – current and future employees, suppliers, distributors
- community groups and pressure groups, including bloggers
- government – central and local
- investors, shareholders and potential sponsors.

2 Carry out research

It can be valuable at this stage to undertake research among your customers or the groups you wish to influence to establish their current awareness of and opinion about your organisation, product or service. This will reveal areas that you need to concentrate on, and can give a benchmark against which to measure your success in meeting your objectives later. It is also important to gain an understanding of the sectors and markets within which the organisation is operating and to find out about trends and issues, past and present, which affect the business and its competitors.

3 Set PR objectives

Objectives outline what you plan to achieve, and strategies describe how you plan to go about it. PR objectives should be closely aligned to the strategy and objectives of the organisation. The objectives you set should be realistic, measurable and time limited. For example, if an organisation aims to increase purchases of product X by consumer group Y by 10% over the next twelve months, a PR objective might be to improve awareness of the benefits of product X among consumer group Y within the next twelve months.

4 Define your key messages

Decide on the messages you wish to get across to the different groups with which your organisation needs to communicate. Outline the concepts you wish to convey – precise wording and presentation can be determined later, when you have chosen your media.

5 Clarify resources

It is important to establish the financial and human resources available for PR activities. Make a list covering budgets, staff, time, equipment, IT requirements, and design and print facilities. Indicate which of these are in-house resources and which may need to be bought in, so that you are in a good position to make clear choices about how to spend your budget.

6 Select a programme of activity

Develop a programme of activities designed to achieve your objectives. This should include a timetable, and can be structured in phases of activity and/or follow a monthly, quarterly or yearly sequence of activities. This programme should clearly prioritise specific stakeholder groups and identify the main communication channels you plan to use.

Some examples of the types of activity you might decide to pursue are listed below. They are outlined under broad headings for ease of access, but some of these activities can also be used in different ways to communicate with different groups of stakeholders. For example, a briefing could be used for public affairs and lobbying, but it could also be used to communicate with potential sponsors, staff and community leaders.

- **Media relations.** Press releases/statements, articles, radio and television interviews and discussions, press conferences and briefings, photo calls and photographs, press visits and press interviews. These may be carried out by telephone, video link, face-to-face, by email or online.

- **Internal communications.** Intranet, email, in-house newsletters, staff briefings and seminars, notice boards, memos, briefing papers, training manuals, internal videos, open days and conferences.

- **Public affairs and lobbying.** Briefing documents for MPs, submissions to government, face-to-face briefings to MPs, parliamentary committees and government ministers, initiating parliamentary questions and tabling early day motions.

- **Events.** Exhibitions, conferences, talks, presentations, road shows, trade-show stands or workshops, competitions and awards.

- **Community relations.** Familiarisation visits, community projects, sponsorship of local charities, open days for community leaders and neighbours, information videos, consultation and discussion groups.

- **Investor relations.** Reports, accounts, AGMs, briefings and presentations, shareholder newspaper, magazine or newsletter, corporate video.

- **Social media.** Tweets, blogs and postings on online networks and community sites.

7 Evaluate successes and failures

Measuring the impact of PR effectively can be challenging, but it will help you to evaluate the success or failure of particular strategies and activities and plan more effectively for the future, as well as enabling you to demonstrate the value of PR to your organisation. Measurement must be SMART, relate to the objectives set and be carried out repeatedly.

It is important to measure outtake and output as well as input and outcome. For example, a measure of whether you met your target for the number of stories released to the media each quarter would be a measure of output; a measure of the extent to which the target audience actually received and understood the message would be a measure of outtake; and a measure of the extent to which the attitudes and behaviour of specific target groups have changed would be a measure of outcome.

A range of techniques can be used, including quantitative and qualitative measures. Opportunities to see (OTS) and gross rating point (GRP) are examples of measures used in PR. OTS is the potential number of occasions an audience can view a relevant item or message about a company in any given period; GRP measures reach against percentage of total population. However, it is important to gain a clear understanding of such measures and their limitations and to interpret the results carefully.

As a manager you should avoid:

- starting to plan without considering who you want to communicate with
- what message you want to put across
- the aims and objectives of the message to be communicated
- which channels will be used
- what activities will be undertaken and when
- what the resourcing costs will be
- how success will be evaluated.

Edward L Bernays
Public relations pioneer

Introduction

Edward Louis Bernays (1891–1995) is widely regarded as an early founder and pioneer in the field of PR and opinion making. Some hail him as the founding father; others contest this accolade, claiming the crown rightly belongs to Ivy Lee, who invented the press release and was responsible for coining the term public relations. What is not contested, however, is the significant contribution Bernays made to PR, which earned him his rightful place in the history books.

During his long and successful career, Bernays demonstrated a pioneering approach to his high-profile campaigns, which were innovative and prolific. He contributed much to the theory of PR, principally by combining traditional journalistic techniques with concepts from the social sciences (psychology and sociology) – something that had not been done before.

Bernays believed that established ideas and opinions could be changed and influenced by those in a trusted position. This was a role he saw himself playing: that of a PR counsel. Through the formulation and development of innovative methods and techniques, he was able to achieve great success for his illustrious clientele, and later he employed his talents to spread his own messages too.

Life and career

Born in Vienna in 1891, Bernays moved to New York the following year. He graduated from Cornell University in 1912 and made New York his home for the rest of his life. Bernays was influenced by the work of his uncle, Sigmund Freud, an eminent psychoanalyst, and adapted his ideas to influence how people thought and behaved within the commercial world. Like Freud, Bernays was born into an influential family, so from a young age he was privy to power and opportunity which would characterise his adult life as well.

In the early years Bernays immersed himself in the role of press agent, working to influence government policy. He expanded and developed the sphere of influence of a press agent far beyond that of his predecessors. He was an ambitious man, seeking to influence not only the government but also the general public.

One of the turning points in the life of the young Bernays was his exposure to the power of propaganda as a means of influencing the public and moulding opinions. He witnessed first hand the effect insightful marketing had on Americans during the First World War, when he was engaged as a foot soldier by the US Committee for Public Information (CPI). He was impressed by the CPI's work, and this fuelled his interest in its marketing techniques and its ability to use them to encourage Americans to support the country's involvement in the war effort. He reasoned that if it was possible to influence attitudes and behaviour in war-time, it could also be achieved during peace-time. Such was the negative war-time connotation of the term 'propaganda' that Bernays sought to influence the public by using the more acceptable term 'public relations', which he continued to promote throughout his life.

In 1919, Bernays founded the first US PR company with Doris Fleischman, whom he later married. They worked together for over 50 years, establishing a profitable and renowned company. In 1923, he published *Crystallizing Public Opinion*, a groundbreaking text in its field. It was the springboard for a long and illustrious career as an expert in his chosen discipline.

Influential clients

Bernays' clientele featured some of the most influential movers and shakers of the day, including US presidents, major enterprises and civil-liberty groups. Among his corporate client list were the American Tobacco Company, Procter & Gamble, General Electric Company, General Motors Corporation and the Waldorf Astoria. As his success grew, so did his reputation and the prestigious clients he attracted. He began to receive recognition and awards for his work and became a sought-after guest speaker at numerous events.

Influential campaigns

Bernays' campaigns won profit and success for many of his clients, yet perhaps the true measure of his expertise and ability to persuade is demonstrated by his ability to change societal attitudes. This required a supreme talent. These challenging and sometimes controversial campaigns were not about increasing product sales or party votes. Bernays was tasked with altering established opinions, attitudes and behaviour, often with the aim of achieving a more democratic US.

In 1920, Bernays became instrumental in a campaign to highlight the civil rights of black Americans when he was asked to orchestrate the publicity surrounding a conference organised by Arthur Spingarn, a civil-rights campaigner. Amid violence and tensions, Bernays and his wife succeeded in bringing to the attention of Americans the need to address the status of black citizens.

An example of a controversial campaign in which Bernays was engaged concerned the taboo of women smoking. Employed by the American Tobacco Company, he campaigned for the right of women to be permitted to smoke in public. This would become a powerful symbol of women's freedom and equality. Bernays' achievement in changing the public's attitude led to the American Tobacco Company's Lucky Strike cigarettes becoming known as 'torches of freedom'. This was a big win for Bernays, demonstrating his ability to change a long-held public view in favour of that of his client.

When the dangers of smoking became known in later years, Bernays performed a complete U-turn when he carried out an anti-smoking campaign during the 1960s. He gained recognition for his work from anti-smoking lobbyists highlighting the dangers of smoking to the public.

Government campaigns

Bernays feared that Americans could easily vote for the 'wrong' person without trusted guidance. He took it upon himself to influence government policy and in turn the public, using his position as a professional opinion former and PR expert to do so. One of his earliest clients was the US Department of War, which asked for his help in persuading companies to employ war veterans.

He was also engaged on behalf of US presidents and political leaders to help spread their message and influence the public to vote in their favour. He worked alongside the White House on one such project to improve President Calvin Coolidge's personal image and the public's opinion of him. Bernays orchestrated a group of popular celebrity figures to dine with the president in an attempt to help American voters see a different side to their leader.

Bernays' connections extended to the First Lady as well; his involvement in the arts industry led to him becoming acquainted with Eleanor Roosevelt – such was his influence. His reach extended beyond US politics, with another of his early clients being the government of Lithuania, which at the time was seeking US recognition.

Innovative PR methods

The nature and subject matter of Bernays' campaigns were as diverse as his client list. He turned his PR talents to ballet,

Broadway, silk and soap with equal enthusiasm. Whatever the context, he employed marketing techniques and methods that were innovative and creative and repeatedly successful in achieving his objective: to change and influence public opinion.

One example was his quest to make the colour green the fashionable choice for women. This came about after women complained that the garish green packaging used for their Lucky Strike cigarettes clashed with their attire. Bernays masterminded an elaborate campaign, which included a charity ball where only green gowns were permitted to be worn. Another example of his creative techniques was on behalf of Procter & Gamble, when he introduced soap-sculpting competitions to engage the public's interest in P&Gs new Ivory soap product.

So what was the secret of Bernays' success? From his early exposure to CPI's successful propaganda efforts, he sought to discover what it was that influenced the public and how this was achieved. He looked to his uncle's work and others engaged in the fields of psychology and social sciences to understand more about thought processes. He also turned his attention to the notion of crowd psychology to help him better understand mass mentality and how he could use this knowledge to exercise wide-scale influence. This winning combination of behavioural sciences and the tried-and-tested journalistic methods of press reporting accounted for the continuing success of Bernays' PR activities.

Endorsements and trust

His successful approach to PR and the promotion of his clients' messages also benefited from his use of endorsements. He partnered with some of the most eminent and well-respected members of the American society of the day because he recognised the importance of endorsements from such trusted household names. He effectively used endorsements to convince the public to follow the lead of prominent Americans and be influenced by them. Today, the use of famous faces to advertise and endorse products and services is common, but Bernays was a pioneer of such tactics, which were new and innovative at the time.

An awareness that people follow those they trust and look up to also underpinned Bernays' PR activities. Based on this, he targeted leaders and those in positions of authority when developing his campaigns. He believed that if he could get the support of authority figures, those they led would automatically follow. This, he maintained, was something that he, as a PR professional, could accomplish; it was not something that a mere ad-man could achieve. Immersed as he was in the era of mass goods production, he nurtured ambitions to achieve the mass distribution of ideas as well.

Surveys

Bernays used surveys to validate opinion and support his campaigns. In the same way as endorsements, the data gathered by surveys helped to give weight to his arguments and encourage the public to share his clients' point of view. His campaign strategy also included using multiple channels to promote the same message. For example, tying radio and newspaper advertising in with one another extended the reach of his messaging.

Bernays' tactics appeared to achieve the impossible: from changing long-established societal opinion to helping General Motors sell cars during the Depression, his success continued despite challenging circumstances and opposition.

In perspective

Bernays claimed that PR can effectively change public opinion and is a necessary aspect of a democratic society in peace-time. Yet his views came under attack when the rise of Fascism demonstrated how the clever use of propaganda could just as easily create a corrupt society. Many of Bernays' peers saw him as greedy and egotistical, and his ambition to become known as the best publicist did little to ingratiate him with his fellow marketers. His constant name-dropping and references to his uncle's fame did not improve matters.

Although Bernays has been criticised over the years, and his status as founding father has been contested, the influence he had on the American public for nine decades cannot be questioned. He laid the foundations for the next generation of marketers and opinion-formers, and many of his ideas and methods are still practised today. His legacy and influence extended beyond the US, his adoptive country, as his ideas became acknowledged around the world.

In his later years, Bernays criticised the discipline of PR. He said with regretful resignation that the skills he employed in successful campaigning were no longer evident in today's approach to PR. He was angered by the emergence of unscrupulous individuals, who he believed were damaging the name of his beloved profession. To address this problem, Bernays spent much time campaigning for PR to be recognised as a profession, calling for it to be licensed and registered. He argued that without the introduction of a licence to practise as a PR professional, the doors would be open to anyone, regardless of education or morals. Despite his many successes for his clients, Bernays' personal campaign for licensing was one that he did not win.

Preparing for a media interview

A media interview is any conversation with a journalist, broadcaster or blogger, whether it is live or recorded, conducted over the phone, by video link or email, or face-to-face. This may include radio or television broadcasts, and interviews with journalists from printed or online publications, or even social media.

Good media coverage, whether it be in the press, trade journals, on radio or television or via newer platforms such as websites, blogs and social media, can be valuable in raising awareness of your organisation, creating a favourable impression and building your reputation. Current technology allows an image or remark to be broadcast to millions instantly, so the media can be powerful and valuable allies – but they can also act as a negative force, destroying relationships of trust and reputations that may have taken years to build up.

You may be reluctant to talk to the media or have had bad experiences in the past. However, doing an interview gives you an opportunity to give your side of the story. If you are nervous or shy, adequate preparation is likely to make you feel more confident. Handling the media effectively can lead to greater awareness of a brand, increased sales of a product or service, enhanced perceptions of an individual or organisation and improved competitive advantage. It can also help you put a message across to a specific audience, explain your position on a topical issue or limit damage in the event of a crisis.

Conversely, handling the media ineffectively can result in a collapse of confidence, a damaged and tarnished reputation, a reduction of influence and respect, confusion, rumour and incorrect or unfair perceptions of a person, product or organisation, missed opportunities or even the end of a profitable business.

The way you handle media contacts, whether proactively or in response to a situation or event, can turn that situation around and create a lasting impression. Doing a successful interview requires clarity and control – it is all too easy to lay yourself open to misunderstanding or misinterpretation, or to be drawn into speaking carelessly and saying things that you later regret. To avoid this, you should plan and prepare carefully and take a calm and measured approach to the interview. This checklist provides guidance on preparing for an interview with the media, with specific guidance for different types of interview conducted across varying media platforms such as radio and television.

Action checklist – general preparation

1 Accept the interview and start to plan for it

Never be rushed into giving an interview. Consider whether the offer is a good opportunity for you and comes from a reputable broadcaster or publication. In most cases, you will want to accept the offer in order to promote your business or put across your version of events. Once you have accepted, it is usually helpful to decide what you want to achieve and then list no more than five points that you want to get across.

When there has been a disaster or a crisis, you may need to step in quickly and at least make a brief comment, even if this not a full in-depth interview. This can put you in a difficult position, as you will have to make some quick decisions about what to say and how to say it. Nevertheless, preparation can still help you, as a good business continuity plan will include guidance on how to deal with the media in emergencies. Stock phrases can be useful, such as: 'Our people are working incredibly hard to resolve this and restore our usual standard of service.'

2 Prepare and anticipate likely or difficult questions

Preparation is a useful way to avoid being tripped up. Consider the following questions:

- What is the focus of media interest? For example, in the case of radio or TV broadcasts, what is the programme about?
- Will the reporter or interviewer be referring to a particular source of information, such as a press release? If so, make sure that you have read this beforehand and are clear about the contents.
- What does the interviewer already know and what do they want to learn?
- How long will your contribution be?
- Who else is being interviewed (e.g. a competitor or customer)?
- Where will the interview take place and who will the interviewer be?
- What questions are you likely to be asked?
- Who is the audience?

As part of your preparation, make sure that you have answers ready for any difficult questions. Do not be afraid of politely challenging questions, assumptions or incorrect information, and make sure that you get back to the points you want to make, rather than being distracted by questions about other topics.

Are you an invited expert or are you defending an action taken by your organisation? This will determine the interviewer's style of questioning, and in the latter case, it is important to clarify in advance with your line manager what you can and cannot say.

3 Make yourself comfortable and establish a rapport with the interviewer

If the interview is taking place outside your home or workplace, try to arrive at the venue early so that you are not rushed and can familiarise yourself with the surroundings. Talk to the interviewer beforehand and attempt to establish a rapport. It is also worth checking your appearance, as this will certainly influence the interviewer, and depending on the type of interview it may also influence the viewer. Calm your nerves by breathing deeply and using whichever relaxation techniques work for you. Focus on your opening sentences and the first main point to get you into the swing of things.

It is important to know what the journalist is seeking from the interview so that you can match their requirements with your own. Understand the journalist's motivation and remember that they have a job to do. Although they may not wish to trip you up, they may well do so inadvertently through lack of care, time or preparation. Remember to focus on your main points and use them as the substance with which to address the questions.

Do not assume that the journalist or your audience possess the same knowledge and information that you do. Keep the message clear and remember your objectives. It is important to avoid using jargon or acronyms, and not to patronise the interviewer or the audience.

4 Project the right image – and do not be hostile

Be friendly, lively and enthusiastic, but do not put on an act. Convey your personality and your message in your tone of voice. It is important to appear confident, remain calm and not to become hostile; in most cases, the journalist is simply trying to elicit information and not to cross-examine you.

If you are being interviewed in relation to a controversy involving your organisation, do not offer excuses or appear defensive. If your organisation has clearly made errors, an apology comes across well. It is not helpful to say 'No comment' or to be unavailable to answer questions. If you wish to take the line that the organisation has now taken action to minimise the likelihood that such an event will happen again, the audience will want specific details or evidence, such as examples or statistics, to prove this.

Beware of entering into informal conversations and giving information off the record. Assume that any information you give to a journalist will be quoted.

5 Develop good relationships with the media

Consider generating your own stories and establishing relationships with the media, rather than seeing interviews as one-offs. The media are frequently undervalued, mistrusted or used only in a crisis: a proactive approach can be of enormous value in establishing understanding and goodwill.

Media training courses have becoming increasingly popular in recent years and may be worth considering if you are in a position where you need to deal with the media regularly. Good media skills courses can help you to gain confidence, overcome fears of making a gaffe and give you practice in handling difficult questions.

Action checklist – press interviews

1 Preparation

Newspaper and magazine interviews carry particular risks, as you are dependent on the journalist's version of events. Ensure that you understand each other, that the facts are correct and that the journalist understands the story.

Find out about:

- the journalist's 'angle' on the story and check that you are happy with it
- the target audience for the interview

- whether others with opposing views to your own will be quoted.

2 The interview

Provide good quotes – the written equivalent of the sound bite.

Remember that the press like to present interesting rather than balanced accounts, and prefer to give examples or tell stories rather than provide general information.

3 Afterwards

You may wish to consider asking to see the article before it is published. Be careful in making this kind of request, however, as it may be considered offensive. Offer to take a call from the journalist later if they wish to double-check any points.

Remember that journalists are people too. If you behave in an agreeable manner and take their needs into consideration, they will (usually) reciprocate. If you are hostile, defensive or obstructive, you are unlikely to get a sympathetic write-up.

Action checklist – radio interviews

1 Preparation

The best times to be on radio are usually 7–9 am, 1–2 pm and 4.30–5.30 pm. If you are able to secure an interview during these times, more people will hear your message. If the reporter is coming to you, choose somewhere quiet, unless the background noise adds particular interest.

You do not need to give the same level of thought to your appearance as with a TV interview, but bear in mind that some radio shows are filmed with a webcam and the footage is streamed live on the internet. In this case at least some of the audience will be able to see you.

2 The interview

Speak with the individual listener in mind. It may be helpful to pick someone you know and picture them. Avoid abstractions. Use vivid, human examples to paint pictures in the listener's mind.

Remember the sound bite. Think up three or four sentences that are particularly quotable and include them, but avoid repetition of words or phrases that risk causing irritation – unless that is what you intend.

If you use notes, make them bullet points and do not read from them. Audiences can tell if you are reading a pre-prepared script. Do not feel under pressure to fill any voids in conversation – the interviewer will manage this.

If the interview is live, you should welcome this as it means your comments cannot be edited in a misleading way. If it is not live, treat it as such to ensure that you get into the right frame of mind.

Do not thump the table, crinkle papers, or clink jewellery.

3 Remote studios and phone-ins

Assume the microphone is live until told otherwise. Listen hard and take notes if you wish; write down callers' names. Answer when it is your turn. Interrupt when necessary and with confidence, or not at all.

Be civil to callers and interviewers, even rude ones, and flatter them: 'That's a fair point, but the real issue here is…'

Action checklist – TV interviews

Some aspects of TV interviews are similar to radio interviews but consider the following additional points.

1 In the studio

Dress appropriately – plain colours, no fussy patterns – and avoid jewellery.

Get used to the environment: arrive early and meet the interviewer if possible. Ask about the line of questioning: what is the first question, etc?

If you are offered make-up, accept it.

2 On location

If you are hosting the crew, find out beforehand what special arrangements they need for the shoot. Talk to the journalist(s) as soon as they arrive. Check that you see the situation the same way, and find out whether they need background information.

Have your own ideas about where you would like to be filmed: consider any distractions and make sure that the background is suitable.

3 During the interview

Sit comfortably, and be friendly and natural. If in doubt, be serious – smiling can be misunderstood. Use positive body language. Do not fidget – relax.

Action checklist – web chats and social-media interviews

1 Preparation

Familiarise yourself with the technology being used. If you are totally unfamiliar with the medium you are using for the web chat, you may need to spend significant time learning about how it works.

If you feel uncomfortable with using the technology, it may be better to decline the invitation, or at least have someone more knowledgeable on hand on the day to help you.

Have a back-up plan in case of any technical difficulties, such as more than one device to access the internet.

Before the interview, check any ground rules or time limits with the interviewer. Ask the interviewer if you can help spread the word about the web chat beforehand, using your own (social) media channels.

2 During the interview

Make sure you are able to type quickly enough to reply to questions rapidly. If you are a slow typist, get a trusted colleague with good typing skills to type the answers you dictate. Remember that people cannot 'hear' your tone of voice online, so be careful in your use of humour.

Web chats are usually informal, but this does not mean that you should not take the time to ensure accurate spelling, grammar and punctuation. Make sure replies are concise and written in an appropriate tone and style for the medium and the audience.

3 Afterwards

Check whether the conversation will be recorded or summarised anywhere and share the link with your networks to give the interview greater reach.

As a manager you should avoid:

- being patronising or using jargon
- becoming hostile, abrasive or flustered
- being rushed into giving an interview or an answer
- assuming the interviewer and audience know about you or your subject
- ignoring the question
- addressing problems – in the case of pre-recorded interviews, ask to do it again if necessary.

Communicating in a crisis

A crisis is any event or situation that has a negative impact on an organisation. Communicating with external and internal audiences at a time of crisis may involve the use of a wide range of media, including the company intranet and website, the press, radio and television broadcasts, and social media.

Whatever form a crisis takes, bad news has a tendency to travel incredibly fast – even more so today with the advent of social media. Rumour and speculation can abound, exaggerating the crisis and distorting the truth, so it is essential to be fully prepared to put your side of the story. There will be little time to think once a crisis hits, but having a crisis communications plan in place before one arises will put you in a better position to offer inquirers an immediate response.

Formulating a crisis communications strategy should form part of, and be integrated with, an organisation's overall business continuity planning activities. Being properly prepared will make it easier for you to correct any misleading impressions and to reassure those affected that you have plans in place to deal with the situation effectively. This could help to save – or at least minimise damage to – your company's operations and reputation, and to retain customer loyalty during the ensuing period of disturbance.

You need to communicate clearly with stakeholders, outlining what the problem is and how you intend to resolve it. The crisis will be handled publicly, especially if the media take an active interest, so you must endeavour to avoid bad publicity by reassuring those concerned that the situation is under control. The appointment of a dedicated spokesperson will ensure that external audiences hear the voice of the organisation, but it is also important to make sure that internal communication is coherent and consistent.

This checklist outlines how to prepare a crisis communications strategy and the steps to take when delivering your message, particularly in the event of a major crisis that cannot be dealt with privately without attracting media attention.

Action checklist

1 Establish a crisis communications team

The size of the team will depend on the size of the organisation. In a large company it should consist of senior managers representing the various organisational divisions, as well as those normally responsible for public relations such as the press officer. Typically headed by the CEO or managing director, acting as the chairperson, the team should also include the heads of IT, HR, marketing, finance, operations, security and health and safety. Take care to include someone with knowledge of and responsibility for the legal side of the business. There should be a dedicated team member with responsibility for keeping records and documenting proceedings.

Allocate responsibilities in the event of a crisis, making sure that team members have a full understanding of their individual duties and how these fit in with the team as a whole.

2 Appoint a spokesperson

The spokesperson communicates the company's message to the public when a crisis breaks, thus becoming the face and voice of the organisation. This is a crucial role, as the public's perception of how an organisation responds to a crisis can significantly affect its reputation. The spokesperson, who will play a central role in damage limitation, may be the head of PR, who will already have experience of dealing with the media and established relationships with journalists, broadcasters and bloggers, or a senior manager who can speak with authority on behalf of the organisation. Whoever is appointed will need to be adept at public speaking, with the ability to communicate to a wide range of different audiences.

It is also advisable to appoint a deputy spokesperson. Depending on the scale and duration of the crisis, and the level of interest it generates, the deputy can support the spokesperson and stand in for them if necessary. This will help to speed up responses to inquirers.

Brief the spokesperson and the deputy as to what they are likely to be required to communicate and the circumstances in which they will need to do so. Provide appropriate training to ensure they have the skills to deliver the all-important public address calmly and confidently. Make sure everyone within the organisation knows who the spokesperson and the deputy are and make their contact details readily available to internal and external audiences.

3 Consider potential risks

Drawing on business impact analysis and risk assessment activities carried out in the course of wider business continuity planning, consider the most likely and most serious scenarios that will require focused communication efforts. The team should convene at regular intervals to review risks and potential or imminent crises, so that questions can be raised promptly and dealt with appropriately.

4 Develop a crisis communications plan

Based on the risks identified, draw up a plan outlining the strategy for responses in the event of a crisis arising and the main steps for handling it.

The plans need to take into account the following:

- the nature of the crisis and who or what is the cause of it
- the scope of the crisis and the level of disruption it will cause – can the business continue to operate?
- those who will be affected – employees, customers, shareholders or other groups
- the likely duration of the crisis
- how the media and other stakeholders are likely to respond.

It will need to cover contingencies for:

- how the crisis will be resolved
- who will need to be informed, including emergency services and public authorities such as those with responsibility for health and safety and the environment
- who will be responsible for handling communications with the various stakeholders
- which communication channels will be used
- what will need to be communicated.

It should also establish what training is required for spokespersons and other employees and whether additional personnel resources will be needed.

As part of the plan, make sure that a briefing on the company and its operations is available. This should cover such matters as what it does, how long it has been in business, who the senior people are and how many employees it has. Do not assume that everyone knows what your company does. Having a briefing document ready can be invaluable for providing background information to the media and other interested parties at short notice. Rehearse and revise the plan regularly, making amendments when necessary.

5 Make arrangements for a control room

When a crisis occurs it is imperative that there is a private and secure room in which the communications team can convene before giving a statement. This should be properly equipped with phone lines, broadband connection, telephones, mobile phones, computers, telephone/videoconferencing facilities, a television, a radio and adequate supplies of stationery. Make briefing notes and copies of the crisis communications plan available for everyone involved and plan to provide refreshments and/or a drinks dispenser for the comfort of the occupants.

If the room is also to act as a media centre for addressing or broadcasting to the public, lighting and sound quality need to be taken into account. The appearance of the room should create the right visual effect, so it must look clean, tidy and professional.

6 Keep communication lines open

In the immediate aftermath of a breaking crisis, it is necessary to ensure that the organisation can easily be contacted by those affected. It is crucial that adequate facilities and sufficient personnel are available to deal with a potential deluge of phone calls, emails and forum postings. It may be necessary to extend opening hours and/or install a 24/7 telephone hotline, for example. Such courses of action will have implications for staffing and training which should have been agreed as part of the crisis communications plan. Check that all lines of external communication are operational: website links, phone lines, email addresses, etc. Make sure that all communication channels are regularly monitored and that inquiries are responded to promptly.

7 Identify your audiences

To communicate effectively, you must identify the recipients and tailor your responses accordingly. Depending on the scale of the crisis, there may be several groups of stakeholders (as well as non-stakeholders) who need to be informed. Stakeholders could include a parent company, employees, investors, customers and suppliers. Non-stakeholders may include the media, regulators/ trade associations, local communities, lobby or special-interest groups, and local and/or central government. If the crisis involves a breach of the law, security or safety, you may need to inform the emergency services. Maintain a database of the key people and their contact details for use in the event of a crisis. This should be checked and updated regularly by a specified member of the crisis communications team.

8 Do not forget to communicate internally

Your employees need to be kept fully informed about the crisis and its impact on them as well as its broader implications; otherwise rumour, uncertainty and speculation will spread, damaging morale and causing unrest and dissatisfaction. Depending on the circumstances, you may need to give instructions about when and where to report for work, reassurances about employees' jobs, or information that will enable them to respond to inquiries and communicate consistently and authoritatively with customers. Be as honest as you can with employees, especially when the outcomes are uncertain; otherwise trust will be undermined.

Provide employees with updates as things progress, preferably face-to-face. Bear in mind that all internal communications via email or the intranet could at some point end up in the public domain. Make sure that messaging is consistent and professional at all times and that the need for complete confidentiality is made clear to everyone. Internal communications need to be handled effectively to ensure the consistency of external messaging.

9 Formulate your response

When a crisis breaks the spokesperson will be required to make a statement. Appropriate messaging is crucial to ensure your organisation presents an accurate account of the situation. The message should provide answers to who, why, where, what, when and how questions. Be consistent in your responses to these questions. Tailor the message to suit difference audiences and what they need to know. For example, customers will want to know when to expect the resumption of deliveries in the event of delays and disruptions. Keep the messages simple and short, leaving no room for misunderstandings, so that audiences get the gist of your communication easily. To be credible, the messages must be truthful and sincere. Do not hesitate to make an apology if it is warranted, but endeavour to deliver a positive message and demonstrate that you are in control of the situation. At the same time, be careful not to make unrealistic promises that you will be unable to keep, and do not pretend that you have all the answers if the facts have not yet been established.

The tone of the message and its immediacy will influence the communication channels chosen for its delivery. Channels include media interviews, press releases, social media, email and telephone. Decide which is the most appropriate for your purpose, taking into account the audience being addressed.

10 Communicate with the media

As part of their public role, your spokesperson will be required to communicate with the media. Journalists could be representing regional or national press, TV or radio. It is essential to put your side of the story across clearly to avoid unnecessary speculation. Communicate promptly as soon as the crisis breaks. Keep the press informed at all times and always be seen to cooperate. Be proactive in instigating contact so that you are not caught off guard. Provide usable quotes and be aware of journalistic deadlines. Share information generously. Return calls promptly and be available for comment. The more cooperative you are, the easier it will be to keep the media on your side.

When speaking to the media, especially in broadcast interviews, remember that body language and attitude convey just as much as the spoken word. Spokespersons need to present themselves well and stay in control of the situation. They need to remain poised. They should be assertive without being aggressive, respond firmly but politely to criticism or provocation and avoid coming across as defensive or evasive, as this will only fuel speculation. It should be decided in advance which subjects they will not discuss (such as profits, punishments, compensation), and they must resist the pressure to make commitments the company may be unable to keep. Lastly, they should communicate openly and honestly and resist the temptation to lie, as this is likely to cause more serious problems in the future.

11 Identify third-party endorsers

In times of crisis it is invaluable to get others to speak well of your organisation. Satisfied customers, suppliers, former employees or trade associations are some of the third-party endorsers you may wish to enlist. Endorsers who can shine a positive light on your company can be particularly helpful if the media appear to be against you. As well as offering positive support to your company, endorsers can validate what the organisation does and how it operates. They can help to circulate and communicate accurate and reliable information to those who are seeking a scoop.

12 Provide employee training

To ensure employees handle things in an appropriate manner, they need the right training. Training is essential in all areas of the business, but especially for those on the front line who will deal with calls and emails and potentially have face-to-face exchanges with affected parties. Frontline employees are also often the most vulnerable to journalists looking for a story.

Make sure employees know what to do in the event of a crisis and have the necessary skills to deal with irate customers or inquisitive outsiders. To ensure consistent messaging to external inquirers, draft a script that can be used for all verbal and written communications. Ensure that employees know to whom to pass inquiries and impress upon them that they must not be drawn into making any comments themselves. Employee training should also incorporate awareness of the crisis communications plan and highlight who is responsible for what.

13 Keep communicating after the crisis

It is important to keep the lines of communication open to restore order as well as reputation. Go back to the external parties on your contact list and update them appropriately; anyone who has been affected will be looking for reassurance that the situation will not reoccur. Thank those who helped to resolve the crisis as well as those who gave loyal support to the business during this troubled period.

Analyse how well the communications plan worked in practice, highlighting lessons learned and any improvements that could be made. Assess how well external and internal audiences were kept informed. Talk to your employees and seek their feedback. Frontline employees are often the first to notice a change in customer attitudes, so their opinions are paramount.

As a manager you should avoid:

- being ill-prepared
- failing to train employees
- appointing an inexperienced spokesperson
- failing to communicate in a timely manner
- failing to engage with the media.

Planning a conference

A conference is a gathering of speakers and delegates, who meet to focus on a particular subject, learn about and discuss issues of mutual interest, solve particular problems, take specific decisions, publicise services to potential markets, or discuss cooperation with other bodies.

The aim of a conference is to bring people together and to provide opportunities for knowledge sharing, networking and finding fresh inspiration. Conferences may be held for promotional, in-company, educational or sales reasons, to name but a few. They may be anything from a half-day event to a residential event that runs for several days, but even the shortest will require extensive planning. A conference can be a memorable and productive event, sparking creative new developments in the field, opening up new opportunities for collaboration, building constructive business relationships, or creating a sense of corporate or professional identity and commitment.

If conferences go wrong, however, they can be costly failures, damaging the reputation of both organisers and host organisations as well as disappointing delegates. It is therefore crucial to take a focused approach to organising conferences to ensure that they meet the desired objectives and outcomes. The difference between success and failure is careful and detailed planning of the whole process, from the setting of objectives to the studious observation of protocol at the final dinner.

This checklist highlights the steps to take and the issues to consider when planning a conference. It concentrates in particular on for-profit events.

Action checklist

1 Decide whether a conference is needed

Planning a conference can be expensive and time-consuming. Ask yourself:

- who you want to reach (delegates)
- what you want to say, ask or discuss, and why
- how and where you want to say it
- how big it will be?

Answering these questions will enable you to determine whether a conference is the most appropriate and cost-effective way of achieving your objectives. It will also help to establish an initial set of objectives for the conference itself, such as how long it will last – a half-day, a full day, or longer.

If, on reflection, a conference does not appear to be the most appropriate option, consider alternatives, particularly the use of technology for webinars or podcasts.

2 Allocate roles and responsibilities

Depending on the size of the conference, there are a number of different ways to plan. You can use a small in-house team or engage an external event management company, for example. Using a small in-house team allows the organisation to be in control and ensures that the plan is agreed internally. Using an event management company can be expensive, especially for smaller events, but it can be cost-effective for large or complex conferences. You must make sure that it is clear who is responsible for what, especially if you appoint an external organiser. If an external organisation is involved, you need to appoint someone in your organisation to act as a point of contact.

The conference manager you appoint bears the ultimate responsibility for the conference's planning and success, and should have experience in dealing with people at all levels and be motivated to manage and promote the conference effectively. The conference manager should:

- understand every detail of what is required and cross-check with the conference team or external organiser regularly
- have full authority to negotiate in relation to the venue and other facilities
- be in contact with all external and internal parties involved.

When there are questions to answer, problems to solve or decisions to take, these should be directed to the conference manager.

3 Agree the budget

Questions to think about when establishing the cost of the conference and the resources required include:

- Has an existing budget already been allocated? If so, how big is it and what does it cover?
- Does the conference aim to make a profit or does it just need to cover its costs?
- Is additional finance required?
- Do you want and will you be able to find sponsorship?
- Is it feasible to raise income by including an exhibition and charging the exhibitors?

4 Set the schedule

Agreed timescales and deadlines need to be agreed with all involved. When setting the schedule bear in mind that you will need to allow sufficient time for:

- setting the date and time of the conference
- selecting a location or venue

- confirming logistical arrangements, e.g. transport, catering, accommodation and other facilities
- identifying, contacting and confirming speakers
- identifying, inviting and registering delegates
- confirming costs – for venue, production, speakers, etc.
- designing, producing and sending out publicity material and contacting advertisers
- ensuring that all legal requirements such as health and safety and public liability insurance are met
- conducting a risk assessment.

The choice of delegates is closely linked to the conference objectives, but it is not always as straightforward as might be imagined. A sales conference, for example, will have salespeople as its delegates, but who else will attend? Will you invite partners? Will you invite customers or potential customers?

5 Select a venue

It takes time to organise a successful conference. If you need to book an external venue for a large conference, you may find that appropriate venues are booked up a year or more in advance. Once the format of the conference, the speakers and the intended delegates have been determined, the conference manager should provide a list of suitable venues which fall within the financial guidelines set by the organisation. Venues can be identified through personal knowledge, word of mouth, venue finders, or placement agencies. When choosing a venue consider the following:

- location – how far will delegates have to travel?
- transport links – road, rail and air
- disability access and facilities
- parking spaces
- sufficient accommodation and facilities for an unknown (although targeted) number of delegates and for staff

- presentation equipment and technology
- space for an accompanying exhibition, if necessary
- access to phones, fax or email and internet access for delegates
- safety measures (exit routes) in case of an emergency
- catering and special diets
- leisure facilities, if required.

It is essential to visit venues to compare them and make sure they meet your specifications. Remember that hotels provide special all-in conference rates and are often cheaper off-season and at weekends. Many universities also operate as conference venues, with upgraded halls of residence providing comfortable accommodation.

When visiting, the conference manager will obviously be given VIP treatment, so take every opportunity to observe how other guests are treated. Also take up references from other organisations, if possible.

The conference room is of prime importance. The size of the room should be the first consideration, but also look for:

- pleasant overall surroundings
- ceiling height in proportion to the size of room (a low ceiling can be oppressive)
- first-class PA system (if it is inadequate, suitable equipment should be hired)
- efficient but quiet air conditioning
- efficient blackout
- easy access for frequent exits and entrances
- comfortable seating
- private rooms for discussion groups, if required.

Check the bedrooms, both standard and executive, to ensure they are clean and have the required facilities. Also check that the catering facilities are adequate to cope with the number of delegates attending. Ask for sample menus, for all requirements, and look at the dining area. Lastly, check how the hotel will deal with sudden arrivals and departures of delegates, or people who arrive in the early hours of the morning. A separate conference reception desk could deal with this problem efficiently, and could also serve as a conference inquiry desk throughout.

6 Approach and book speakers

You will need to identify a list of potential speakers. These should be experienced, sincere and convincing people with good presentation skills, who will be able to gain and hold the attention and interest of the audience. Remember that even if the material is first-class, poor presentation skills can sabotage a conference session. Approach the speakers and try to confirm the bookings as quickly as possible. Once a booking is confirmed, agree the content and format of each speaker's presentation. It is advisable to approach and book reserve speakers, too, in case there are any last-minute problems.

Remember to stress and re-stress the timing of the presentations, as most speakers tend to overrun. At least one dress rehearsal is advisable – schedule a date and ensure the speakers can attend. Consider issuing an information pack for your speakers to reinforce the timings and details. If you are not paying your speakers, consider providing appropriate gifts and invitations to any formal end-of-conference dinner, and so on.

7 Draw up the programme

The business programme (drawn up by the conference organising team) should meet your objectives completely. Plan the presentation schedule to ensure the attention of delegates is held (people usually concentrate for a maximum of twenty to thirty minutes before needing a break). In the programme allow for:

- breaks between the heavier presentations

- extended refreshment breaks
- light lunches to prevent delegates from dozing off in the afternoon session (if serving alcohol, do so in moderation)
- a few 'light relief' presentations sandwiched between any heavier ones
- the right balance between interactive, lecturing and discussion sessions
- the right balance between work and leisure.

Consider drawing up a social programme, as both organisers and delegates will benefit from staying together for most, if not all, of the conference period.

8 Work out logistical details

- How will delegates register on arrival?
- Who will staff the information desk to answer delegates' queries?
- How will catering be handled (if not provided by the venue)?
- Where are private rooms located (if required)?

Establishing the right atmosphere is crucial. There is no guaranteed formula to guide you but, clearly, panic and a last-minute rush are to be avoided. Calm efficiency, courtesy and friendliness should help to set the right tone.

During the conference, the manager needs to concentrate solely on the administration of the event and the domestic needs of the delegates. He or she should also have an assistant and sufficient support staff.

9 Make contingency plans

It is important to have contingency plans in place to cover eventualities such as extreme weather conditions, illness of key personnel or speakers, travel disruptions, etc. Think through what problems might arise and how they might be handled. Consider what unexpected circumstances would lead you to cancel or postpone the event and how delegates would be informed.

10 Advertise the conference

Once you are clear about people you wish to attend and have confirmed details of the date, venue and speakers, you can start to advertise the conference. The conference team should have already considered the best channels to target the relevant groups of people and identified possible advertisers. It is essential to advertise as widely and accurately as possible.

Invitations and reminders should be sent out at intervals to gain maximum exposure, and joining instructions issued in good time for delegates to make any necessary arrangements.

11 Provide an information pack for delegates

Prepare an information pack for delegates containing:

- conference objectives
- details of the programme
- information on facilities available to delegates
- the guest list
- speaker profiles
- information on the conference sponsors
- relevant and appropriate flyers and advertising material
- a feedback/evaluation form.

When the conference ends, organise a debriefing with the conference manager and team. Evaluate how successful the event was and whether your objectives were met. Identify any problems that arose and the lessons to be learned for next time. Assess all the feedback received from delegates. Produce a checklist of action points for the next conference.

As a manager you should avoid:

- failing to draw up a contingency plan to cover the unexpected

- worrying about being too perfectionist – check and recheck details as often as you can
- leaving anything to chance or assumption
- being too cautious about making changes to the conference plan, if these will ensure success
- neglecting to get feedback from delegates for later analysis and review.

Acknowledgements

The Chartered Management Institute (CMI) would like to thank the members of our Subject Matter Experts group for their generous contribution to the development of the management checklists. This panel of 80 members and fellows of CMI and its sister institute, the Institute of Consulting, draw on their knowledge and expertise to provide feedback on the currency, relevance and practicality of the advice given in the checklists. A full listing of the subject matter experts is available at www.managers.org.uk/about-us/work-with-us/as-a-subject-matter-expert.

This book has been made possible by the work of CMI's staff, in particular Catherine Baker, Colleen Bihanycz, Piers Cain, Sarah Childs, Michelle Jenkins, Robert Orton, Alex Palmer, Nick Parker, Karen Walsh and Mary Wood, the Series Editor. We would also like to thank Stephen Brough, Paul Forty and Clare Grist Taylor of Profile Books for their support.

The management checklists are based on resources available online at www.managers.org.uk to CMI members to assist them in their work and career development, and to subscribers to the online resource portal ManagementDirect.

Index